New International Version

THE BOOK OF

Isaiah

FROM THE
New International Version

ZONDERVAN BIBLE PUBLISHERS

OF THE ZONDERVAN CORPORATION
GRAND RAPIDS, MICHIGAN 49506

Preface

THIS preliminary translation of Isaiah is part of the New International Version of the Holy Bible. In 1973 the NIV New Testament appeared. Since then, work has been continuing on the Old Testament, which is scheduled for publication in 1978.

The New International Version is neither a paraphrase nor a revision of any previous translation, but a new translation made directly from the original languages. In the Old Testament the Masoretic Text (the traditional Hebrew text) has been generally followed, except where the Dead Sea Scrolls, the Septuagint and other ancient versions, variant manuscript readings and internal evidence have led to corrections in the Masoretic Text.

A transdenominational effort, the New International Version involves over a hundred Biblical scholars from the English-speaking world. All of them are committed to the belief that the Bible is the inspired Word of God. Their aim is to make a translation that is clear and idiomatic, contemporary but not quickly dated, dignified but not stilted. They are therefore seeking simplicity of expression together with sensitive regard for the connotation and sound of the words chosen. Literary stylists work with them in pursuit of this aim.

Where there is uncertainty about the wording of the original text or its precise meaning, footnotes call attention to this. Although sectional headings are inserted in the translation to facilitate reference, they are not an official part of the text. In addition, bullets have been inserted in some proper nouns between two adjacent vowels (e.g., Mo·ab) to indicate that both vowels should be pronounced.

The Committee on Bible Translation expresses its gratitude to the New York International Bible Society for underwriting the heavy cost of producing the New International Version. The Committee welcomes suggestions and criticisms, which may be sent to the New York International Bible Society at 5 East 48th Street, New York, New York 10017.

Upon request the Society will forward a list of translators and literary consultants associated with the project.

To the praise and glory of God we now offer this portion of the Old Testament of the New International Version.

The Committee on Bible Translation

THE BOOK OF
Isaiah

Isaiah

1 The vision concerning Judah and Jerusalem that Isaiah son of Amoz saw during the reigns of Uzziah, Jotham, Ahaz and Hezekiah, kings of Judah.

A Rebellious Nation

2Hear, O heavens! Listen, O earth!
   For the LORD has spoken:
"I reared children and brought them up,
   but they have rebelled against me.
3The ox knows his master,
   the donkey his owner's manger,
but Israel does not know,
   my people do not understand."

4Ah, sinful nation,
   a people loaded with guilt,
a brood of evildoers,
   children given to corruption.
They have forsaken the LORD;
   they have spurned the Holy One of Israel
   and turned their backs on him.

5Why should you be beaten anymore?
   Why do you persist in rebellion?
Your whole head is injured,
   your whole heart afflicted.
6From the sole of your foot to the top of your
    head

there is no soundness—
only wounds and welts
and open sores,
not cleansed or bandaged
or soothed with oil.

⁷Your country is desolate,
your cities burned with fire;
your fields are being stripped by foreigners
right before you,
laid waste as when overthrown by strangers.
⁸The Daughter of Zion is left
like a shelter in a vineyard,
like a hut in a field of melons,
like a city under siege.
⁹Unless the LORD Almighty
had left us some survivors,
we would have become like Sodom,
we would have been like Gomorrah.

¹⁰Hear the word of the LORD,
you rulers of Sodom;
listen to the law of our God,
you people of Gomorrah!
¹¹"The multitude of your sacrifices—
what are they to me?" says the LORD.
"I have more than enough of burnt offerings,
of rams and fattened animals;
I have no pleasure
in the blood of bulls and lambs and goats.
¹²When you come to meet with me,
who has asked this of you,
this trampling of my courts?
¹³Stop bringing meaningless offerings!
Your incense is detestable to me.
New Moons, Sabbaths and convocations—
I cannot bear your evil assemblies.

¹⁴Your New Moon festivals and your appointed
       feasts
    my soul hates.
  They have become a burden to me,
    I am weary of bearing them.
¹⁵When you spread out your hands in prayer,
    I will hide my eyes from you;
  even if you offer many prayers,
    I will not listen.
  Your hands are full of blood;
¹⁶   wash and make yourselves clean.
  Take your evil deeds
    out of my sight!
  Stop doing wrong,
¹⁷   learn to do right!
  Pursue justice,
    encourage the oppressed.ᵃ
  Defend the cause of the fatherless,
    plead the case of the widow.

¹⁸"Come now, let us reason together,"
    says the LORD.
  "Though your sins are like scarlet,
    they shall be as white as snow;
  though they are red as crimson,
    they shall be like wool.
¹⁹If you are willing and obedient,
    you will eat the best from the land;
²⁰but if you resist and rebel,
    you will be devoured by the sword."
         For the mouth of the LORD has spoken.

²¹See how the faithful city has become a harlot!
    She once was full of justice;
  righteousness used to dwell in her—

ᵃ 17 Or *reprove the oppressor.*

but now murderers!
²²Your silver has become dross,
    your choice wine is diluted with water.
²³Your rulers are rebels,
    companions of thieves;
they all love bribes
    and chase after gifts.
They do not defend the cause of the fatherless;
    the widow's case does not come before
      them.
²⁴Therefore the Lord, the Lorᴅ Almighty,
    the Mighty One of Israel, declares:
"Ah, I will get relief from my foes
    and avenge myself on my enemies.
²⁵I will turn my hand against you;
    I will thoroughly purge away your dross
    and remove your impurities.
²⁶I will restore your judges as in days of old,
    your counselors as at the beginning.
Afterward you will be called
    The City of Righteousness,
    The Faithful City."

²⁷Zion will be redeemed with justice,
    her penitent ones with righteousness.
²⁸But rebels and sinners will both be broken
      together,
    and those who forsake the Lord will perish.

²⁹"You will be ashamed because of the sacred oaks
    in which you have delighted;
you will be disgraced because of the gardens
    that you have chosen.
³⁰You will be like an oak with fading leaves,
    like a garden without water.
³¹The mighty man will become tinder
    and his work a spark;

both will burn together,
with no one to quench the fire."

The Mountain of the LORD

2 This is what Isaiah son of Amoz saw concerning Judah
and Jerusalem.

²In the last days

the mountain of the LORD's temple will be
established
as chief among the mountains;
it will be raised above the hills,
and all nations will stream to it.

³Many peoples will come and say,

"Come, let us go up to the mountain of the LORD,
to the house of the God of Jacob.
He will teach us his ways,
so that we may walk in his paths."
The law will go out from Zion,
the word of the LORD from Jerusalem.
⁴He will judge between the nations
and will settle disputes for many peoples.
They will beat their swords into plowshares
and their spears into pruning hooks.
Nation will not take up sword against nation,
nor will they train for war anymore.

⁵Come, O house of Jacob,
let us walk in the light of the LORD!

The Day of the LORD

⁶You have abandoned your people,
the house of Jacob.
They are full of superstitions from the east;
they practice divination like the Philistines

5

and clasp hands with pagans.
⁷Their land is full of silver and gold;
　　there is no end to their treasures.
　Their land is full of horses;
　　there is no end to their chariots.
⁸Their land is full of idols;
　　they bow down to the work of their hands,
　　to what their fingers have made.
⁹So men will be brought low
　　and people humbled—
　but do not raise them up.*a*

¹⁰Go into the rocks,
　　hide in the ground
　from dread of the LORD
　　and the splendor of his majesty!
¹¹The eyes of the arrogant man will be humbled
　　and the pride of men brought low;
　the LORD alone will be exalted in that day.

¹²The LORD Almighty has a day in store
　　for all the proud and lofty,
　　for all that is exalted
　　(and they will be humbled),
¹³for all the cedars of Lebanon, tall and lofty,
　　and all the oaks of Bashan,
¹⁴for all the towering mountains
　　and all the high hills,
¹⁵for every lofty tower
　　and every fortified wall,
¹⁶for every trading ship*b*
　　and every stately vessel.
¹⁷The arrogance of man will be brought low
　　and the pride of men humbled;
　the LORD alone will be exalted in that day,
¹⁸　and the idols will totally disappear.

---

a 9 Or *not forgive them.*　　*b* 16 Hebrew *every ship of Tarshish*

¹⁹Men will flee to caves in the rocks
>and to holes in the ground
from dread of the LORD
>and the splendor of his majesty,
>when he rises to shake the earth.
²⁰In that day men will throw away
>to the rodents and bats
their idols of silver and idols of gold,
>which they made to worship.
²¹They will flee to caverns in the rocks
>and to the overhanging crags
from dread of the LORD
>and the splendor of his majesty,
>when he rises to shake the earth!
²²Stop trusting in man,
>who has but a breath in his nostrils.
Of what account is he?

Judgment on Jerusalem and Judah

3 See now, the Lord,
>the LORD Almighty,
is about to take from Jerusalem and Judah
>both supply and support:

all supplies of food and all supplies of water,
² the hero and warrior,
the judge and prophet,
>the soothsayer and elder,
³the captain of fifty and man of rank,
>the counselor, skilled craftsman and clever
>>enchanter.
⁴I will make boys their officials:
>mere children will govern them.
⁵People will oppress each other—
>man against man, neighbor against neighbor.
The young will rise up against the old,
>the base against the honorable.

⁶A man will seize one of his brothers
    at his father's home, and say,
"You have a cloak, you be our leader;
    take charge of this heap of ruins!"
⁷But in that day he will cry out,
    "I have no remedy.
I have no food or clothing in my house;
    do not make me the leader of the people."

⁸Jerusalem staggers,
    Judah is falling;
their words and deeds are against the LORD,
    defying his glorious presence.
⁹The look on their faces testifies against them;
    they parade their sin like Sodom;
    they do not hide it.
Woe to them!
    They have brought disaster upon themselves.

¹⁰Tell the righteous it will be well with them,
    for they will enjoy the fruit of their deeds.
¹¹Woe to the wicked!
    Disaster is upon them!
They will be paid back
    for what their hands have done.
¹²Youths oppress my people,
    women rule over them.
O my people, your guides lead you astray;
    they turn you from the path.

¹³The LORD takes his place in court;
    he rises to judge the people.
¹⁴The LORD enters into judgment
    against the elders and leaders of his people:
"It is you who have ruined my vineyard;
    the plunder from the poor is in your houses.

¹⁵What do you mean by crushing my people
and grinding the faces of the poor?"
declares the Lord, the LORD Almighty.

¹⁶The LORD says,
"The women of Zion are haughty,
walking along with outstretched necks,
flirting with their eyes,
tripping along with mincing steps,
with ornaments jingling on their ankles.
¹⁷Therefore the Lord will bring sores on the heads
of the women of Zion;
the LORD will make their scalps bald."

¹⁸In that day the Lord will snatch away their finery: the bangles and headbands and crescent necklaces, ¹⁹the earrings and bracelets and veils, ²⁰the headdresses and ankle chains and sashes, the perfume bottles and charms, ²¹the signet rings and nose rings, ²²the fine robes and the capes and cloaks and purses, ²³the mirrors and linen garments and tiaras and shawls.

²⁴Instead of fragrance there will be a
stench;
instead of a sash, a rope;
instead of well-dressed hair, baldness;
instead of fine clothing, sackcloth;
instead of beauty, branding.
²⁵Your men will fall by the sword,
your warriors in battle.
²⁶The gates of Zion will lament and mourn;
destitute, she will sit on the ground.

4 In that day seven women will take hold of one man and say, "We will eat our own food and provide our own clothes, only let us be called by your name. Take away our disgrace!"

The Branch of the LORD

²In that day the Branch of the LORD will be beautiful and glorious, and the fruit of the land will be the pride and glory of the survivors in Israel. ³Those who are left in Zion, who remain in Jerusalem, will be called holy, all who are recorded among the living in Jerusalem. ⁴The Lord will wash away the filth of the women of Zion; he will cleanse the bloodstains from Jerusalem by a spirit*ᵃ* of judgment and a spirit*ᵃ* of fire. ⁵Then the LORD will create a canopy over all of Mount Zion and over those who assemble there, a cloud of smoke by day and a glow of flaming fire by night. ⁶It will be a shelter and shade from the heat of the day, and a refuge and hiding place from the storm and rain.

The Song of the Vineyard

5 I will sing to the one I love
    a song about his vineyard:
My loved one had a vineyard
    on a fertile hillside.
²He dug it up and cleared it of stones
    and planted it with the choicest vines.
He built a watchtower in it
    and cut out a winepress as well.
Then he looked for a crop of good grapes,
    but it yielded only bad fruit.

³"Now you dwellers in Jerusalem and men of
    Judah,
    judge between me and my vineyard.
⁴What more could have been done for my
    vineyard
    than I have done for it?
When I looked for good grapes,
    why did it only yield bad?
⁵Now I will tell you

ᵃ4 Or *the Spirit*

what I am going to do to my vineyard:
I will take away its hedge,
    and it will be destroyed;
I will break down its wall,
    and it will be trampled.
⁶I will make it a wasteland,
    neither pruned nor cultivated,
    and briers and thorns will grow there.
I will command the clouds
    not to rain on it."

⁷The vineyard of the LORD Almighty
    is the house of Israel,
and the men of Judah
    are the garden of his delight.
And he looked for justice, but saw bloodshed;
    for righteousness, but heard cries of distress!

Woes and Judgments

⁸Woe to you who add house to house
    and join field to field,
till no space is left
    and you live alone in the land.

⁹The LORD Almighty has declared in my hearing:

"Surely the great houses will become desolate,
    the fine mansions left without occupants.
¹⁰A ten-acreᵃ vineyard will produce only a few
        gallonsᵇ of wine,
    six bushelsᶜ of seed only half a busheld of
        grain."

¹¹Woe to those who rise early in the morning

a 10 Hebrew *ten-yoke*, that is, the land plowed by 10 yoke of oxen in one day
b 10 Hebrew *one bath*; a bath probably equals about 6 gallons
c 10 Hebrew *one homer*; a homer probably equals about 6 bushels
d 10 Hebrew *one ephah*; an ephah was 1/10 of a homer

to run after their drinks,
who stay up late at night
till they are inflamed with wine.
¹²They have harps and lyres at their banquets,
tambourines and flutes and wine,
but they have no regard for the deeds of the
LORD,
no respect for the work of his hands.
¹³Therefore my people will go into exile
for lack of understanding;
their men of rank will die of hunger
and their masses will be parched with thirst.
¹⁴Therefore the grave*a* enlarges its appetite
and opens its mouth without limit;
into it will descend their nobles and masses
with all their brawlers and revelers.
¹⁵Both low and high will be humbled
and the eyes of the arrogant will be brought
low.
¹⁶But the LORD Almighty will be exalted by his
justice,
the holy God will show himself holy by his
righteousness.
¹⁷Then sheep will graze as in their own pasture;
lambs will feed*b* among the ruins of the rich.

¹⁸Woe to those who draw sin along with cords of
deceit,
and wickedness as with cart ropes,
¹⁹to those who say, "Let God hurry,
let him hasten his work
so we may see it.
Let it approach,
let the plan of the Holy One of Israel come,
so we may know it."

---

a 14 Hebrew *Sheol*   *b* 17 Septuagint; Hebrew *strangers will eat*

²⁰Woe to those who call evil good
   and good evil,
who put darkness for light
   and light for darkness,
who put bitter for sweet
   and sweet for bitter.

²¹Woe to those who are wise in their own eyes
   and clever in their own sight.

²²Woe to those who are heroes at drinking wine
   and champions at mixing drinks,
²³who acquit the guilty for a bribe,
   but deny justice to the innocent.

²⁴Therefore as tongues of fire lick up straw
   and as dry grass sinks down in the flames,
so their roots will decay
   and their flowers blow away like dust,
for they have rejected the law of the LORD
      Almighty
   and spurned the word of the Holy One of
      Israel.
²⁵Therefore the LORD's anger burns against his
      people,
   and his hand is raised to strike them down;
the mountains shake,
   and the dead bodies are like refuse in the
      streets.

Yet for all this, his anger is not turned away,
   his hand is still upraised.

²⁶He lifts up a banner for the distant nations,
   he whistles for those at the ends of the earth.
Here they come,
   swiftly and speedily!

²⁷Not one of them grows tired or stumbles,
    not one slumbers or sleeps;
not a belt is loosened at the waist,
    not a sandal thong is broken.
²⁸Their arrows are sharp,
    all their bows are strung;
their horses' hoofs seem like flint,
    their chariot wheels like a whirlwind.
²⁹Their roar is like that of the lion,
    they roar like young lions;
they growl as they seize their prey
    and carry it off with none to rescue.
³⁰In that day they will roar over it
    like the roaring of the sea.
And if one looks at the land,
    he will see darkness and distress;
    even the light will be darkened by the clouds.

Isaiah's Commission

6 In the year that King Uzziah died, I saw the Lord seated on a throne, high and exalted, and the train of his robe filled the temple. ²Above him were seraphs, each with six wings: With two wings they covered their faces, with two they covered their feet, and with two they were flying. ³And they were calling to one another:

    "Holy, holy, holy is the Lord Almighty;
    the whole earth is full of his glory."

⁴At the sound of their voices the doorposts and thresholds shook, and the temple was filled with smoke.

⁵"Woe to me!" I cried. "I am ruined! For I am a man of unclean lips, and I live among a people of unclean lips, and my eyes have seen the King, the Lord Almighty."

⁶Then one of the seraphs flew to me, with a live coal in his hand, which he had taken with tongs from the altar. ⁷With it he touched my mouth and said, "See, this has

touched your lips; your guilt is taken away and your sin atoned for."

⁸Then I heard the voice of the Lord saying, "Whom shall I send? And who will go for us?"

And I said, "Here am I. Send me!"

⁹He said, "Go and tell this people:

'Be ever hearing, but never understanding;
  be ever seeing, but never perceiving.'
¹⁰Make the heart of this people calloused
  make their ears dull,
  and close their eyes.ᵃ
Otherwise they might see with their eyes,
  hear with their ears,
  understand with their hearts,
  and turn and be healed."

¹¹Then I said, "For how long, O Lord?"
And he answered:

"Until the cities lie ruined
  and without inhabitant,
until the houses are left deserted
  and the fields ruined and ravaged;
¹²until the LORD has sent everyone far away,
  and the land is utterly forsaken.
¹³And though a tenth remains in the land,
  it will again be laid waste.
But as the terebinth and oak
  leave stumps when they are cut down,
  so the holy seed will be the stump in the
    land."

ᵃ 9,10 Hebrew; Septuagint 'You will be ever hearing, but never understanding;
      you will be ever seeing, but never perceiving.'
    ¹ᐞThis people's heart has become calloused;
      they hardly hear with their ears,
      and they have closed their eyes.

The Sign of Immanuel

7 When Ahaz son of Jotham son of Uzziah was king of Judah, King Rezin of Syria[a] and Pekah son of Remaliah, king of Israel, marched up to fight against Jerusalem, but they could not overpower it.

²Now the house of David was told, "Syria[a] has allied itself with[b] Ephra·im"; so the hearts of Ahaz and his people were shaken, as the trees of the forest are shaken by the wind.

³Then the LORD said to Isaiah, "Go out, you and your son She·ar-Jashub,[c] to meet Ahaz at the end of the aqueduct of the Upper Pool, on the road to the Washerman's Field. ⁴Say to him, 'Be careful, keep calm and don't be afraid. Do not lose heart because of these two smoldering stubs of firewood —because of the fierce anger of Syria[a] and of the son of Remaliah. ⁵Syria,[a] Ephra·im and Remaliah's son have plotted your ruin, saying, ⁶"Let us invade Judah; let us tear it apart and divide it among ourselves, and make the son of Tabe·el king over it." ⁷Yet this is what the Sovereign LORD says:

It will not take place,
    it will not happen.
⁸For the head of Syria[a] is Damascus,
    and the head of Damascus is only Rezin.
Within sixty-five years
    Ephra·im will be too shattered to be a people.
⁹The head of Ephra·im is Samaria,
    and the head of Samaria is only Remaliah's son.
If you do not stand firm in your faith,
    you will not stand at all!' "

¹⁰Again the LORD spoke to Ahaz, ¹¹"Ask the LORD your God for a sign, whether in the deepest depths or in the highest heights."

---

a 1,2,4,5,8 Hebrew Aram   b 2 Or has set up camp in
c 3 She·ar-Jashub means a remnant will return.

¹²But Ahaz said, "I will not ask; I will not put the LORD to the test."

¹³Then Isaiah said, "Hear now, you house of David! Is it not enough to try the patience of men? Will you try the patience of my God also? ¹⁴Therefore the Lord himself will give you*a* a sign: A virgin will be with child and will give birth to a son, and*b* will call him Immanuel.*c* ¹⁵He will eat curds and honey when he knows enough to reject the wrong and choose the right. ¹⁶But before the boy knows enough to reject the wrong and choose the right, the land of the two kings you dread will be laid waste. ¹⁷The LORD will bring on you and on your people and on the house of your father a time unlike any since Ephra·im broke away from Judah—he will bring the king of Assyria."

¹⁸In that day the LORD will whistle for flies from the distant streams of Egypt and for bees from the land of Assyria. ¹⁹They will all come and settle in the steep ravines and in the crevices in the rocks, on all the thornbushes and at all the water holes. ²⁰In that day the Lord will use a razor hired from beyond the River*d*—the king of Assyria—to shave your head and the hair of your legs, and to take off your beards also. ²¹In that day, a man will keep alive a young cow and two goats. ²²And because of the abundance of the milk they give, he will have curds to eat. All who remain in the land will eat curds and honey. ²³In that day, in every place where there were a thousand vines worth a thousand silver shekels, there will only be briers and thorns. ²⁴Men will go there with bows and arrows, for the land will be covered with briers and thorns. ²⁵As for all the hills once cultivated by the hoe, you will no longer go there for fear of the briers and thorns; they will become places where cattle are turned loose and where sheep run.

---

a 14 The Hebrew is plural.   *b 14* Masoretic Text; Dead Sea Scrolls *and he* or *and they*   *c 14 Immanuel* means *God with us.*   *d 20* That is, the Euphrates

Assyria, the LORD's Instrument

8 The LORD said to me, "Take a large scroll and write on it with an ordinary pen: Maher-Shalal-Hash-Baz.[a] [2]And I will call in Uriah the priest and Zechariah son of Jeberechiah as reliable witnesses for me."

[3]Then I went to the prophetess, and she conceived and gave birth to a son. And the LORD said to me, "Name him Maher-Shalal-Hash-Baz.[a] [4]Before the boy knows how to say 'My father' or 'My mother,' the wealth of Damascus and the plunder of Samaria will be carried off by the king of Assyria."

[5]The LORD spoke to me again:

> [6]"Because this people has rejected
> the gently flowing waters of Shiloah
> and rejoices over Rezin
> and the son of Remaliah,
> [7]therefore the Lord is about to bring against them
> the mighty flood waters of the River[b]—
> the king of Assyria with all his pomp.
> It will overflow all its channels,
> run over all its banks
> [8]and sweep on into Judah, swirling over it,
> passing through it and reaching up to the
> neck.
> His outspread wings will cover the breadth of
> your land,
> O Immanuel[c]!"

> [9]Raise the war cry,[d] you nations, and be shattered!
> Listen, all you distant lands.
> Prepare for battle, and be shattered!
> Prepare for battle, and be shattered!
> [10]Devise your strategy, but it will be thwarted;

---

a 1,3 *Maher-Shalal-Hash-Baz* means *quick to the plunder, swift to the spoil.*
b 7 That is, the Euphrates   c 8 *Immanuel* means *God with us.*
d 9 Or *Do your worst,*

propose your plan, but it will not stand,
for God is with us.[a]

Fear God

[11]The LORD spoke to me with his strong hand upon me, warning me not to follow the way of this people. He said:

[12]"Do not call conspiracy
everything that these people call conspiracy;[b]
do not fear what they fear,
and do not dread it.
[13]The LORD Almighty is the one you are to regard
as holy,
he is the one you are to fear,
he is the one you are to dread.
[14]And he will be a sanctuary,
but for both houses of Israel he will be
a stone that causes men to stumble
and a rock that makes them fall,
and for the people of Jerusalem he will be
a trap and a snare.
[15]Many of them will stumble;
they will fall and be broken,
and be snared and be captured."

[16]Bind up the testimony
and seal up the law among my disciples.
[17]I will wait for the LORD,
who is hiding his face from the house of
Jacob.
I will put my trust in him.

[18]Here am I, and the children the LORD has given me—we are signs and symbols in Israel from the LORD Almighty, who dwells on Mount Zion.

[a] 10 Hebrew *Immanuel*
[b] 12 Or *Do not call for a treaty*
  every time these people call for a treaty;

¹⁹When men tell you to consult mediums and spiritists, who whisper and mutter, should not a people consult their God? Why consult the dead on behalf of the living? ²⁰To the law and to the testimony! If they do not speak according to this word, they have no light of dawn. ²¹Distressed and hungry, they will roam through the land; when they are famished, they will become enraged and, looking upward, will curse their king and their God. ²²Then they will look toward the earth and see only distress and darkness and fearful gloom, and they will be thrust into utter darkness.

To Us a Child Is Born

9 Nevertheless, there will be no more gloom for those who were in distress. In the past he humbled the land of Zebulun and the land of Naphtali, but in the future he will honor Galilee of the Gentiles, by the way of the sea, along the Jordan—

²The people walking in darkness
    have seen a great light;
on those living in the land of the shadow of
    death[a]
    a light has dawned.
³You have enlarged the nation
    and increased their joy;
they rejoice before you
    as people rejoice at the harvest,
as men rejoice
    when dividing the plunder.
⁴For as in the day of Midian's defeat,
    you have shattered
the yoke that burdens them,
    the bar across their shoulders,
    the rod of their oppressor.
⁵Every warrior's boot used in battle

a 2 Or *land of darkness*

and every garment rolled in blood
will be destined for burning,
   will be fuel for the fire.
⁶For to us a child is born,
   to us a son is given,
   and the government will be on his shoulders.
And he will be named
   Wonderful Counselor,ᵃ Mighty God,
   Everlasting Father, Prince of Peace.
⁷Of the extension of his government and peace
   there will be no end.
He will reign on David's throne,
   and over his kingdom,
establishing and upholding it
   with justice and righteousness
   from that time on and forever.
The zeal of the Lᴏʀᴅ Almighty
   will accomplish this.

The LORD's Anger Against Israel

⁸The Lord has sent a message against Jacob;
   it will fall on Israel.
⁹All the people will know it—
   Ephra·im and the inhabitants of Samaria—
who say with pride
   and arrogance of heart,
¹⁰"The bricks have fallen down,
   but we will rebuild with dressed stone;
the sycamores have been felled,
   but we will replace them with cedars."
¹¹But the Lᴏʀᴅ has strengthened Rezin's foes
   against them
   and has spurred their enemies on.
¹²Syriansᵇ from the east and Philistines from the
   west

ᵃ6 Or *Wonderful, Counselor,*   ᵇ12 Hebrew *Aram*

have devoured Israel with open mouth.

Yet for all this, his anger is not turned away,
  his hand is still upraised.

13But the people have not returned to him who
    struck them,
  nor have they sought the LORD Almighty.
14So the LORD will cut off from Israel both head
    and tail,
  both palm branch and reed in a single day;
15the elders and prominent men are the head,
  the prophets who teach lies are the tail.
16Those who guide this people mislead them,
  and those who are guided are led astray.
17Therefore the Lord will take no pleasure in the
    young men,
  nor will he pity the fatherless and widows,
for everyone is ungodly and wicked,
  every mouth speaks vileness.

Yet for all this, his anger is not turned away,
  his hand is still upraised.

18Surely wickedness burns like a fire;
  it consumes briers and thorns,
it sets the forest thickets ablaze—
  so that it rolls upward in a column of
    smoke.
19By the wrath of the LORD Almighty
  the land will be scorched,
and the people will be fuel for the fire;
  no one will spare his brother.
20On the right they will devour,
  but still be hungry;
on the left they will eat,
  but not be satisfied.

Each will feed on the flesh of his own offspring[a]:
21 Manasseh will feed on Ephra·im, and Ephra·im
    on Manasseh;
    together they will turn against Judah.

Yet for all this, his anger is not turned away,
    his hand is still upraised.

10

Woe to those who make unjust laws,
    to those who issue oppressive decrees,
2to deprive the poor of their rights
    and rob my oppressed people of justice,
making widows their prey
    and robbing the fatherless.
3What will you do on the day of reckoning,
    when disaster comes from afar?
To whom will you run for help?
    Where will you leave your riches?
4Nothing will remain but to cringe among the
    captives
    or fall among the slain.

Yet for all this, his anger is not turned away,
    his hand is still upraised.

God's Judgment on Assyria

5Woe to the Assyrian, the rod of my anger,
    in whose hand is the club of my wrath!
6I send him against a godless nation,
    I dispatch him against a people who anger me,
to seize loot and snatch plunder,
    and to trample them down like mud in the streets.
7But this is not what he intends,
    this is not what he has in mind;
his purpose is to destroy,
    to put an end to many nations.

a 20 Or *arm*

⁸"Are not my commanders all kings?" he says.
⁹   "Has not Calno fared like Carchemish?
Is not Hamath like Arpad,
    and Samaria like Damascus?
¹⁰As my hand seized the kingdoms of the idols,
    kingdoms whose images excelled those of
        Jerusalem and Samaria—
¹¹shall I not deal with Jerusalem and her images
    as I dealt with Samaria and her idols?"

¹²When the Lord has finished all his work against Mount Zion and Jerusalem, he will say, "I will punish the king of Assyria for the willful pride of his heart and the haughty look in his eyes. ¹³For he says:

'By the strength of my hand I have done this,
    and by my wisdom, because I have
        understanding.
I removed the boundaries of nations,
    I plundered their treasures;
    like a mighty one I subdued^a their kings.
¹⁴As one reaches into a nest,
    so my hand reached for the wealth of the
        nations;
as men gather abandoned eggs,
    so I gathered all the countries;
not one flapped a wing,
    or opened its mouth to chirp.' "

¹⁵Does the ax raise itself above him who swings it,
    or the saw boast against him who uses it?
As if a rod were to wield him who lifts it up,
    or a club brandish him who is not wood!
¹⁶Therefore, the Lord, the LORD Almighty,
    will send a wasting disease upon his sturdy
        warriors;

^a 13 Or *treasures; I subdued the mighty,*

under his pomp a fire will be kindled
like a blazing flame.
¹⁷The Light of Israel will become a fire,
their Holy One a flame;
in a single day it will burn and consume
his thorns and his briers.
¹⁸The splendor of his forests and fertile fields,
it will completely destroy—
as when a sick man wastes away.
¹⁹And the remaining trees of his forests will be so
few
that a child could write them down.

The Remnant of Israel

²⁰In that day the remnant of Israel,
the survivors of the house of Jacob,
will no longer rely on him
who struck them down,
but will truly rely on the LORD,
the Holy One of Israel.
²¹A remnant will return,[a] a remnant of Jacob,
will return to the Mighty God.
²²Though your people, O Israel, should be like the
sand by the sea,
only a remnant will return.[a]
Destruction has been decreed,
overwhelming and righteous.
²³The Lord, the LORD Almighty, will carry out
the destruction decreed upon the whole land.

²⁴Therefore, this is what the Lord, the LORD Almighty,
says,

"O my people who live in Zion,
do not be afraid of the Assyrians,

---

a 21, 22 Hebrew *She·ar-Jashub*

who beat you with a rod
and lift up a club against you, as Egypt did.
²⁵Very soon, my anger against you will end
and my wrath will be directed to their
destruction."

²⁶The Lord Almighty will lash them with a whip,
as when he struck down Midian at the rock of
Oreb;
and he will raise his rod over the waters,
as he did in Egypt.
²⁷In that day their burden will be lifted from your
shoulders,
their yoke from your neck;
the yoke will be broken
because you have grown so fat.ᵃ

²⁸They enter Aiath;
they pass through Migron;
they store supplies at Michmash.
²⁹They go over the pass, and say,
"We will camp overnight at Geba."
Ramah trembles;
Gibeah of Saul flees.
³⁰Cry out, O Daughter of Gallim!
Listen, O Laishah!
Poor Anathoth!
³¹Madmenah is in flight;
the people of Gebim take cover.
³²This day they will halt at Nob;
they will shake their fist
at the mount of the Daughter of Zion,
at the hill of Jerusalem.

³³See, the Lord, the Lord Almighty,
will lop off the boughs with great power.

ᵃ 27 Hebrew; Septuagint *broken from your shoulders*

The lofty trees will be felled,
the tall will be brought low.
³⁴He will cut down the forest thickets with an ax;
Lebanon will fall before the Mighty One.

The Branch From Jesse

11 A shoot will come up from the stump of Jesse;
from his roots a Branch will bear fruit.
²The Spirit of the LORD will rest on him—
the Spirit of wisdom and of understanding,
the Spirit of counsel and of power,
the Spirit of knowledge and of the fear of the
LORD—
³and he will delight in the fear of the LORD.

He will not judge by what he sees with his eyes,
or decide by what he hears with his ears;
⁴but with righteousness he will judge the needy,
with justice he will give decisions for the poor
of the earth.
He will strike the earth with the rod of his
mouth;
with the breath of his lips he will slay the
wicked.
⁵Righteousness will be his belt
and faithfulness the sash around his waist.

⁶The wolf will live with the lamb,
the leopard will lie down with the goat,
the calf and the lion and the yearlingᵃ together;
and a little child will lead them.
⁷The cow will feed with the bear,
their young will lie down together,
and the lion will eat straw like the ox.
⁸The infant will play near the hole of the cobra,

ᵃ6 Hebrew; some ancient versions *lion will feed*

and the young child put his hand into the
viper's nest.
⁹They will neither harm nor destroy
in all my holy mountain,
for the earth will be full of the knowledge of the
LORD
as the waters cover the sea.

¹⁰In that day the Root of Jesse will stand as a banner for
the peoples; the nations will rally to him, and his place of rest
will be glorious. ¹¹In that day the Lord will reach out his hand
a second time to reclaim the remnant that is left of his people
from Assyria, from Lower Egypt, from Upper Egypt,ᵃ from
Cush,ᵇ from Elam, from Babylonia,ᶜ from Hamath and from
the islands of the sea.

¹²He will raise a banner for the nations
and gather the exiles of Israel;
he will assemble the scattered people of Judah
from the four quarters of the earth.
¹³Ephra·im's jealousy will vanish,
and Judah's enemiesᵈ will be cut off;
Ephra·im will not be jealous of Judah,
nor Judah hostile toward Ephra·im.
¹⁴They will swoop down on the slopes of Philistia
to the west;
together they will plunder the people to the
east.
They will lay hands on Edom and Mo·ab,
and the Ammonites will be subject to them.
¹⁵The LORD will dry up
the gulf of the Egyptian sea;
with a scorching wind he will sweep his hand
over the Euphrates River.ᵉ

ᵃ11 Hebrew *Pathros*   ᵇ11 That is, ancient Ethiopia   ᶜ11 Hebrew *Shinar*
ᵈ13 Or *hostility*   ᵉ15 Hebrew *the River*

He will break it up into seven streams
    so that men can cross over in sandals.
16There will be a highway for the remnant of his
      people
    that is left from Assyria,
as there was for Israel
    when they came up from Egypt.

Songs of Praise

12 In that day you will say:

"I will praise you, O LORD.
    Although you were angry with me,
your anger has turned away
    and you have comforted me.
2Surely God is my salvation;
    I will trust and not be afraid.
The LORD, the LORD, is my strength and my
      song;
    he has become my salvation."
3With joy you will draw water
    from the wells of salvation.

4In that day you will say:

"Praise the LORD,
    call on his name;
make known among the nations what he has
      done,
    and proclaim that his name is exalted.
5Sing to the LORD, for he has done glorious
      things;
    let this be known to all the world.
6Shout aloud and sing for joy, people of Zion,
    for great is the Holy One of Israel among
      you."

A Prophecy Against Babylon

13 An oracle concerning Babylon that Isaiah son of Amoz saw:

²Raise a banner on a bare hilltop,
    shout to them;
  beckon to them
    to enter the gates of the nobles.
³I have commanded my holy ones;
    I have summoned my warriors to carry out my
        wrath,
    those who rejoice in my triumph.

⁴Listen, a noise on the mountains,
    like that of a great multitude!
  Listen, an uproar among the kingdoms,
    like nations massing together!
  The LORD Almighty is mustering
    an army for war.
⁵They come from faraway lands,
    from the ends of the heavens—
  the LORD and the weapons of his wrath—
    to destroy the whole country.

⁶Wail! For the day of the LORD is near;
    it will come like a destructive blow from the
        Almighty.ᵃ
⁷Because of this, all hands will go limp,
    every man's heart will melt.
⁸Terror will seize them,
    pain and anguish will grip them;
    they will writhe like a woman in labor.
  They will look aghast at each other,
    their faces aflame.

ᵃ 6 Hebrew *Shaddai*

⁹See, the day of the LORD is coming
   —a cruel day, with wrath and burning anger—
to make the land desolate
   and destroy the sinners within it.
¹⁰The stars of heaven and their constellations
   will not show their light.
The rising sun will be darkened,
   and the moon will not give its light.
¹¹I will punish the world for its evil,
   the wicked for their sins.
I will put an end to the arrogance of the haughty
   and will humble the pride of the ruthless.
¹²I will make man scarcer than pure gold,
   more rare than the gold of Ophir.
¹³Therefore I will make the heavens tremble;
   and the earth will shake from its place
at the wrath of the LORD Almighty,
   in the day of his burning anger.

¹⁴Like hunted antelope,
   like sheep without a shepherd,
each will return to his own people,
   each will flee to his native land.
¹⁵Whoever is captured will be thrust through;
   all who are caught will fall by the sword.
¹⁶Their infants will be dashed to pieces before
      their eyes;
   their houses will be looted and their wives
      ravished.

¹⁷See, I will stir up against them the Medes,
   who do not care for silver
   and have no delight in gold.
¹⁸Their bows will strike down the young men;
   they will have no mercy on infants,
   nor will they look with compassion on
      children.

¹⁹Babylon, the jewel of kingdoms,
     the glory of the Chaldeans'^a pride,
will be overthrown by God
     like Sodom and Gomorrah.
²⁰She will never be inhabited
     or lived in through all generations;
no Arab will pitch his tent there,
     no shepherd will rest his flocks there.
²¹But desert creatures will lie there,
     owls will fill her houses;
there the ostriches will dwell,
     and there the wild goats will leap about.
²²Hyenas will howl in her strongholds,
     jackals in her luxurious palaces.
Her time is at hand,
     and her days will not be prolonged.

14 The Lord will have compassion on Jacob;
     once again he will choose Israel
     and will settle them in their own land.
Aliens will join them
     and will unite with the house of Jacob.
²Nations will take them
     and bring them to their own place.
And the house of Israel will possess the nations
     as menservants and maidservants in the
          Lord's land.
They will make captives of their captors
     and rule over their oppressors.

³On the day the Lord gives you relief from suffering and turmoil and cruel bondage, ⁴you will take up this taunt against the king of Babylon:

     How the oppressor has come to an end!
     How his fury^b has ended!

---

^a19 That is, Babylonians'   ^b4 Dead Sea Scrolls and some ancient versions; the meaning of the word in the Masoretic Text is uncertain.

⁵The LORD has broken the rod of the wicked,
    the scepter of the rulers,
⁶which in anger struck down peoples
    with unceasing blows,
 and in fury subdued nations
    with relentless aggression.
⁷All the lands are at rest and at peace;
    they break into singing.
⁸Even the pine trees and the cedars of Lebanon
    exult over you and say,
 "Now that you have been laid low,
    no woodsman comes to cut us down."

⁹The grave*ᵃ* below is all astir
    to meet you at your coming;
 it arouses the spirits of the departed to greet
    you—
    all those who were leaders in the world;
 it makes them rise from their thrones—
    all those who were kings over the nations.
¹⁰They will all respond,
    they will say to you,
 "You also have become as weak as we are;
    you have become like us!"

¹¹All your pomp has been brought down to the
    grave,*ᵃ*
    along with the noise of your harps;
 maggots are spread out beneath you
    and worms cover you.
¹²How you have fallen from heaven,
    O morning star, son of the dawn!
 You have been cast down to the earth,
    you who once laid low the nations!

ᵃ 9,11 Hebrew *Sheol*

¹³You said in your heart,
"I will ascend to heaven;
I will raise my throne
above the stars of God;
I will sit enthroned on the mount of assembly,
on the utmost heights of the sacred mountain.^a
¹⁴I will ascend above the tops of the clouds;
I will make myself like the Most High."
¹⁵But you are brought down to the grave,^b
to the depths of the pit.

¹⁶Those who see you stare at you,
they ponder your fate:
"Is this the man who shook the earth
and made kingdoms tremble,
¹⁷the man who made the world a desert,
who overthrew its cities
and would not let his captives go home?"

¹⁸All the kings of the nations lie in state,
each in his own tomb.
¹⁹But you are cast out of your tomb,
like a rejected branch;
you are covered with the slain,
with those pierced by the sword,
those who descend to the stones of the pit.
Like a corpse trampled underfoot,
²⁰   you will not join them in burial,
for you have destroyed your land
and killed your people.

The offspring of the wicked
will never be mentioned again.
²¹Prepare a place to slaughter his sons
for the sins of their forefathers;

---

^a13 Or *the north*; Hebrew *Zaphon*   ^b15 Hebrew *Sheol*

they are not to rise to inherit the land
    and cover the earth with their cities.

²²"I will rise up against them,"
    declares the Lord Almighty.
"I will cut off from Babylon her name and
        survivors,
    her offspring and descendants,"
                        declares the Lord.
²³"I will turn her into a place for owls
    and into swampland,
I will sweep her with the broom of destruction,"
    declares the Lord Almighty.

A Prophecy Against Assyria

²⁴The Lord Almighty has sworn,

"Surely, as I have planned, so it will be,
    and as I have purposed, so it will stand.
²⁵I will crush the Assyrian in my land;
    on my mountains I will trample him down.
His yoke will be taken from my people,
    and his burden removed from their shoulders."

²⁶This is the plan determined for the whole world;
    this is the hand stretched out over all nations.
²⁷For the Lord Almighty has purposed, and who
        can thwart him?
    His hand is stretched out, and who can turn it
        back?

A Prophecy Against the Philistines

²⁸This oracle came in the year King Ahaz died:

²⁹Do not rejoice, all you Philistines,
    that the rod that struck you is broken;
from the root of that snake will spring up a
        viper,

its fruit will be a darting, venomous serpent.
³⁰The poorest of the poor will find pasture,
    and the needy will lie down in safety.
But your root I will destroy by famine;
    it will slay your survivors.

³¹Wail, O gate! Howl, O city!
    Melt away, all you Philistines!
A cloud of smoke comes from the north,
    and there is not a straggler in its ranks.
³²What answer shall be given
    to the envoys of that nation?
"The LORD has established Zion,
    and in her his afflicted people will find
        refuge."

A Prophecy Against Mo·ab

15 An oracle concerning Mo·ab:

Ar in Mo·ab is ruined,
    destroyed in a night!
Kir in Mo·ab is ruined,
    destroyed in a night!
²Dibon goes up to its temple,
    to its high places to weep;
    Mo·ab wails over Nebo and Medeba.
Every head is made bald,
    and every beard cut off.
³In the streets they wear sackcloth;
    on the roofs and in the public squares
they all wail,
    prostrate with weeping.
⁴Heshbon and Ele·aleh cry out,
    their voices are heard all the way to Jahaz.
Therefore the armed men of Mo·ab cry out,
    and their hearts are faint.

⁵My heart cries out over Mo·ab;
    her fugitives flee as far as Zo·ar,
    as far as Eglath Shelishiyah.
They go up the way to Luhith,
    weeping as they go;
on the road to Horona·im
    they lament their destruction.
⁶The waters of Nimrim are dried up
    and the grass is withered;
the vegetation is gone
    and nothing green is left.
⁷So all that they have acquired and stored up
    they carry away over the Ravine of the
      Poplars.
⁸Their outcry echoes along the border of Mo·ab;
    their wailing reaches as far as Egla·im,
    their lamentation as far as Be·er Elim.
⁹Dimon's*ᵃ* waters are full of blood,
    but I will bring still more upon Dimon*ᵃ* —
a lion upon the fugitives of Mo·ab
    and upon those who remain in the land.

16 Send lambs as tribute
    to the ruler of the land,
from Sela, across the desert,
    to the mount of the Daughter of Zion.
²Like fluttering birds
    pushed from the nest,
so are the women of Mo·ab
    at the fords of the Arnon.

³"Give us counsel,
    render a decision.
Make your shadow like night—
    at high noon.

ᵃ 9 Masoretic Text; Dead Sea Scrolls and Vulgate *Dibon*

Hide the fugitives,
    do not betray the refugees.
⁴Let the Mo·abite fugitives stay with you;
    be their shelter from the destroyer."

For the oppressor will come to an end,
    and destruction will cease;
    the aggressor will vanish from the land.
⁵In love a throne will be established;
    in faithfulness a man will sit on it—
    one from the house*a* of David—
one who in judging seeks justice,
    and speeds the cause of righteousness.

⁶We have heard of Mo·ab's pride—
    his overweening pride and conceit,
his pride and his insolence—
    but his boasts are empty.
⁷Therefore the Mo·abites wail,
    they wail together for Mo·ab.
Lament and grieve
    for the raisin cakes of Kir Hareseth.
⁸The fields of Heshbon wither,
    the vines of Sibmah also.
The rulers of the nations
    have trampled down the choicest vines,
which once reached Jazer
    and spread toward the desert.
Their shoots spread out
    and went as far as the sea.
⁹So I weep, as Jazer weeps,
    for the vines of Sibmah.
O Heshbon, O Ele·aleh,
    I drench you with tears!
The shouts of joy over your ripened fruit

a 5 Hebrew *tent*

and over your harvests have been stilled.
¹⁰Joy and gladness are gone from the orchards;
    no one sings or shouts in the vineyards;
no one treads out wine at the presses,
    for I have put an end to the shouting.
¹¹My heart laments for Mo·ab like a harp,
    my inmost being for Kir Hareseth.
¹²When Mo·ab appears at his high place,
    he only wears himself out;
when he goes to his shrine to pray,
    it is to no avail.

¹³This is the word the LORD has already spoken concerning Mo·ab. ¹⁴But now the LORD says: "Within three years, as a servant bound by contract would count them, Mo·ab's splendor and all his many people will be despised, and his survivors will be very few and feeble."

An Oracle Against Damascus

17 An oracle concerning Damascus:

"See, Damascus will no longer be a city,
    but will become a heap of ruins,
²The cities of Aro·er will be deserted
    and left to flocks, which will lie down,
    with no one to make them afraid.
³The fortified city will disappear from Ephra·im,
    and royal power from Damascus;
the remnant of Syria*ᵃ* will be
    like the glory of the Israelites,"
                  declares the LORD Almighty.

⁴"In that day the glory of Jacob will fade;
    the fat of his body will waste away.
⁵It will be as when a reaper gathers the standing
    grain

ᵃ 3 Hebrew *Aram*

and harvests the grain with his arm—
as when a man gleans heads of grain
in the Valley of Repha·im.
⁶Yet some gleanings will remain,
as when an olive tree is beaten,
leaving two or three olives on the topmost
branches,
four or five on the fruitful boughs,"
declares the LORD, the God of Israel.

⁷In that day men will look to their Maker
and turn their eyes to the Holy One of Israel.
⁸They will not look to the altars,
the work of their hands,
and they will have no regard for the Asherah
poles
and the incense altars their fingers have made.

⁹In that day their strong cities, which they left because of
the Israelites, will be like places abandoned to thickets and
underbrush. And all will be desolation.

¹⁰For you have forgotten the God who saves you;
you have not remembered the Rock, your
fortress.
Therefore, though you set out the finest plants
and plant imported vines—
¹¹though in the day you set them out, you make
them grow,
and on the morning when you plant them, you
bring them to bud,
yet the harvest will be as nothing
in the day of disease and incurable pain.

¹²Oh, the raging of many nations—
they rage like the raging sea!
Oh, the uproar of the peoples—
they roar like the roaring of great waters!

¹³Although the peoples roar like the roar of
    surging waters,
  when he rebukes them they flee far away,
driven before the wind like chaff on the hills,
  like tumbleweed before a gale.
¹⁴In the evening, sudden terror!
  Before the morning, they are gone!
This is the portion of those who loot us,
  the lot of those who plunder us.

A Prophecy Against Cush

18 Woe to the land of whirring wings*ᵃ*
    along the rivers of Cush,*ᵇ*
  ²which sends envoys by sea
    and in papyrus boats over the water.

  Go, swift messengers,
  to a people smooth-skinned and tall,
    to a people feared far and wide,
  an aggressive nation of strange speech,
    whose land is divided by rivers.

  ³All you people of the world
    and you who live on the earth,
  when a banner is raised on the mountains,
    you will see it,
  and when a trumpet sounds,
    you will hear it.
  ⁴This is what the LORD says to me:
    "I will remain quiet and will look on from my
      dwelling place,
  like shimmering heat in the sunshine,
    like a cloud of dew in the heat of harvest."
  ⁵For, before the harvest, when the blossom is
      gone

ᵃ 1 Or *of locusts*   ᵇ 1 That is, ancient Ethiopia

and the flower becomes a ripening grape,
he will cut off the shoots with pruning knives,
and cut down and take away the spreading
branches.
⁶They will all be left to the mountain birds of
prey
and to the wild animals;
the birds will feed on them all summer,
the wild animals all winter.

⁷At that time gifts will be brought to the LORD Almighty

from a people smooth-skinned and tall
from a people feared far and wide,
an aggressive nation of strange speech,
whose land is divided by rivers—

the gifts will be brought to Mount Zion, the place of the
Name of the LORD Almighty.

A Prophecy About Egypt

19 An oracle concerning Egypt:

See, the LORD rides on a swift cloud
and is coming to Egypt.
The idols of Egypt tremble before him,
and the hearts of the Egyptians melt within
them.

²"I will stir up Egyptian against Egyptian—
brother will fight against brother,
neighbor against neighbor,
city against city,
kingdom against kingdom.
³The Egyptians will lose heart,
and I will bring their plans to nothing;
they will consult the idols and the spirits of the
dead,

the mediums and the spiritists.
⁴I will hand the Egyptians over
   to the power of a cruel master,
and a fierce king will rule over them,"
   declares the Lord, the Lᴏʀᴅ Almighty.

⁵The waters of the river will dry up,
   and the riverbed will be parched and dry.
⁶The canals will stink;
   the streams of Egypt will decline and dry up.
The reeds and rushes will wither,
⁷   also the plants along the Nile,
   at the mouth of the river.
Every sown field along the Nile
   will become parched, will blow away and be
      no more.
⁸The fishermen will groan and lament,
   all who cast hooks into the Nile;
those who throw nets on the water
   will pine away.
⁹Those who work with combed flax will despair,
   the weavers of fine linen will lose hope.
¹⁰The workers in cloth will be dejected,
   and all the wage earners will be sick at heart.

¹¹The officials of Zo·an are nothing but fools;
   the wise counselors of the Pharaoh give stupid
      advice.
How can you say to the Pharaoh,
   "I am one of the wise men,
   a disciple of the ancient kings"?

¹²Where are your wise men now?
   Let them show you and make known
what the Lᴏʀᴅ Almighty
   has planned against Egypt.
¹³The officials of Zo·an have become fools,

the leaders of Memphis*a* are deceived;
the cornerstones of her peoples
have led Egypt astray.
¹⁴The Lord has poured into them
a spirit of dizziness;
they make Egypt stagger in all that she does,
as a drunkard staggers around in his vomit.
¹⁵There is nothing Egypt can do—
head or tail, palm branch or reed.

¹⁶In that day the Egyptians will be like women. They will shudder with fear at the uplifted hand that the Lord Almighty raises against them. ¹⁷And the land of Judah will bring terror to the Egyptians; everyone to whom Judah is mentioned will be terrified, because of what the Lord Almighty is planning against them.

¹⁸In that day five cities in Egypt will speak the language of Canaan and swear allegiance to the Lord Almighty. One of them will be called the City of Destruction.*b*

¹⁹In that day there will be an altar to the Lord in the heart of Egypt, and a monument to the Lord at its border. ²⁰It will be a sign and witness to the Lord Almighty in the land of Egypt. When they cry out to the Lord because of their oppressors, he will send them a savior and defender, and he will rescue them. ²¹So the Lord will make himself known to the Egyptians, and in that day they will acknowledge the Lord. They will worship with sacrifices and grain offerings; they will make vows to the Lord and keep them. ²²The Lord will strike Egypt with a plague; he will strike them and heal them. They will turn to the Lord, and he will respond to their pleas and heal them.

²³In that day there will be a highway from Egypt to Assyria. The Assyrians will go to Egypt and the Egyptians to Assyria. The Egyptians and Assyrians will worship

*a*13 Hebrew *Noph*   *b*18 Most MSS of the Masoretic Text; Dead Sea Scrolls, some ancient versions and some Masoretic MSS *City of the Sun* (that is, *Heliopolis*)

44

together. ²⁴In that day Israel will be the third, along with Egypt and Assyria, a blessing in the earth. ²⁵The LORD Almighty will bless them, saying, "Blessed be Egypt my people, Assyria my handiwork, and Israel my heritage."

A Prophecy Against Egypt and Cush

20In the year that the supreme commander, sent by Sargon king of Assyria, came to Ashdod and attacked and captured it— ²at that time the LORD spoke through Isaiah son of Amoz. He said to him, "Take off the sackcloth from your body and the sandals from your feet." And he did so, going around stripped and barefoot.

³Then the LORD said, "Just as my servant Isaiah has gone stripped and barefoot for three years, as a sign and portent against Egypt and Cush,[a] ⁴so the king of Assyria will lead away stripped and barefoot the Egyptian captives and Cushite exiles, young and old, with buttocks bared—to Egypt's shame. ⁵Those who trusted in Cush[a] and boasted in Egypt will be afraid and put to shame. ⁶In that day the people who live on this coast will say, 'See what has happened to those we relied on, those we fled to for help and deliverance from the king of Assyria! How then can we escape?' "

A Prophecy Against Babylon

21 An oracle concerning the Desert by the Sea:

Like whirlwinds sweeping through the
     southland,
   an invader comes from the desert,
   from a land of terror.

²A dire vision has been shown to me:
   The traitor betrays, the looter takes loot.
 Elam, attack! Media, lay siege!
   I will bring to an end all the groaning she
     caused.

[a] 3,5 That is, ancient Ethiopia

³At this my body is racked with pain,
    pangs seize me, like those of a woman in
      labor;
I am staggered by what I hear,
    I am bewildered by what I see.
⁴My heart falters,
    fear makes me tremble;
the twilight I longed for
    has become a horror to me.

⁵They set the tables,
    they spread the rugs,
    they eat, they drink!
Get up, you officers,
    oil the shields!

⁶For this is what the Lord says to me:

"Go, post a lookout
    and have him report what he sees.
⁷When he sees chariots
    with teams of horses,
riders on donkeys
    or riders on camels,
let him be alert,
    fully alert."

⁸And the lookout[a] shouted,

"Day after day, my lord, I stand on the
    watchtower;
    every night I stay at my post.
⁹Look, here comes a man in a chariot
    with a team of horses.
And he gives back the answer:
    'Babylon has fallen, has fallen!
All the images of its gods
    lie shattered on the ground!' "

a 8 Dead Sea Scrolls and Syriac; Masoretic Text *A lion*

¹⁰O my people, crushed on the threshing
floor,
    I tell you what I have heard
from the LORD Almighty,
    from the God of Israel.

A Prophecy Against Edom

¹¹An oracle concerning Dumah[a]:

Someone calls to me from Seir,
    "Watchman, what is left of the night?
    Watchman, what is left of the night?"
¹²The watchman replies,
    "Morning is coming, but also the night.
If you would ask, then ask;
    and come back yet again."

A Prophecy Against Arabia

¹³An oracle concerning Arabia:

You caravans of Dedanites,
    who camp in the thickets of Arabia,
¹⁴   bring water for the thirsty;
you who live in Tema,
    bring food for the fugitives.
¹⁵They flee from the sword,
    from the drawn sword,
from the bent bow
    and from the heat of battle.

¹⁶This is what the Lord says to me: "Within one year, as
a servant bound by contract would count it, all the pomp of
Kedar will come to an end. ¹⁷The survivors of the bowmen,
the warriors of Kedar, will be few." The LORD, the God of
Israel, has spoken.

---

[a] 11 Dumah means *silence* or *stillness,* a word play on Edom.

A Prophecy About Jerusalem

22 An oracle concerning the Valley of Vision:

What troubles you now,
     that you have all gone up on the housetops,
²O town full of commotion,
     O city of tumult and revelry?
Your slain were not killed by the sword,
     nor did they die in battle.
³All your leaders have fled together;
     they have been captured without using the
          bow.
All you who were caught were taken prisoner
          together,
     having fled while the enemy was still far
          away.
⁴Therefore I said, "Turn away from me;
     let me weep bitterly!
Do not try to console me
     over the destruction of my people."

⁵The Lord, the LORD Almighty, has a day
     of tumult and trampling and terror
     in the Valley of Vision,
a day of battering down walls
     and of crying out to the mountains.
⁶Elam takes up the quiver,
     with her charioteers and horses;
     Kir uncovers the shield.
⁷Your choicest valleys are full of chariots,
     and horsemen are posted at the city gates;
⁸   the defenses of Judah are stripped away.

And you looked in that day
     to the weapons in the Palace of the Forest;
⁹you saw that the City of David
     had many breaches in its defenses;

you stored up water
    in the Lower Pool.
¹⁰You counted the buildings in Jerusalem
    and tore down houses to strengthen the wall.
¹¹You built a reservoir between the two walls
    for the water of the Old Pool,
but you did not look to the One who did it,
    or have regard for the One who planned it
        long ago.

¹²The Lord, the LORD Almighty,
    called you on that day
to weep and to wail,
    to tear out your hair and put on sackcloth.
¹³But see, there is joy and revelry,
    slaughtering of cattle and killing of sheep,
    eating of meat and drinking of wine!
"Let us eat and drink," you say,
    "for tomorrow we die!"

¹⁴The LORD Almighty has revealed this in my hearing: "Till your dying day this sin will not be atoned for," says the Lord, the LORD Almighty.

¹⁵This is what the Lord, the LORD Almighty, says:

"Go, say to this steward,
    to Shebna, who is in charge of the palace:
¹⁶What are you doing here and who gave you
        permission
    to cut out a grave for yourself here,
hewing your grave on the height
    and chiseling your resting place in the rock?

¹⁷"Beware, the LORD is about to take firm hold of
        you
    and hurl you away, O you mighty man.
¹⁸He will roll you up tightly like a ball

and throw you into a large country.
There you will die
and there your splendid chariots will remain—
you disgrace to your master's house!
¹⁹I will depose you from your office,
and they will oust you from your position.

²⁰"In that day I will summon my servant, Eliakim son of Hilkiah. ²¹I will clothe him with your robe and fasten your sash around him and hand your authority over to him. He will be a father to those who live in Jerusalem and to the house of Judah. ²²I will place on his shoulder the key to the house of David; what he opens no one can shut, and what he shuts no one can open. ²³I will drive him like a peg into a firm place; he will be a seat*ᵃ* of honor for the house of his Father. ²⁴All the glory of his family will hang on him: its offspring and offshoots—all its lesser vessels, from the bowls to all the jars.

²⁵"In that day," declares the LORD Almighty, "the peg driven into the firm place will give way; it will be sheared off and will fall, and the load hanging on it will be cut down." The LORD has spoken.

A Prophecy About Tyre

23 An oracle concerning Tyre:

Wail, O ships of Tarshish!
For Tyre is destroyed,
and left without house or harbor.
From the land of Cyprusᵇ
word has come to them.

²Be silent, you people of the island
and you merchants of Sidon,
whom the seafarers have enriched.

ᵃ 23 Or *throne*   *ᵇ* 1 Hebrew *Kittim*

³On the great waters
  came the grain of the Shihor;ᵃ
the harvest of the Nile was the revenue of Tyre,
  and she became the marketplace of the nations.

⁴Be ashamed, O Sidon, also you, O fortress of the
    sea,
  for the sea has spoken:
"I have neither been in labor nor given birth;
  I have neither reared sons nor brought up
    daughters."
⁵When word comes to Egypt,
  they will be in anguish at the report from
    Tyre.

⁶Cross over to Tarshish;
  wail, you people of the island.
⁷Is this your city of revelry,
  the old, old city,
whose feet have taken her
  to settle in far-off lands?
⁸Who purposed this against Tyre,
  the bestower of crowns,
whose merchants are princes,
  whose traders are renowned in the earth?
⁹The Lord Almighty purposed it,
  to bring low the pride of all glory,
  and to humble all who are renowned in the
    earth.

¹⁰Go through your land;ᵇ
  the daughter of Tarshish, like the Nile,

ᵃ 2,3 Masoretic Text; one Dead Sea Scroll
    who cross over the sea;
    your envoys ³ are on the great waters.
    The grain of the Shihor,
ᵇ 10 Masoretic Text; Dead Sea Scrolls and Septuagint *Till your land;*

will no longer be a haven for you.[a]

11The LORD has stretched out his hand over the sea
and made its kingdoms tremble.
He has given an order concerning Phoenicia[b]
that her fortresses be destroyed.
12He said, "No more of your reveling,
O Virgin Daughter of Sidon, now crushed!

"Up, cross over to Cyprus[c];
even there you will find no rest."
13Look at the land of the Chaldeans,[d]
this people that is now of no account!
The Assyrians have made it
a place for desert creatures;
they raised up their siege towers,
they stripped its palaces bare
and turned it into a ruin.

14Wail, you ships of Tarshish;
your fortress is destroyed!

15At that time Tyre will be forgotten for seventy years, the
span of a king's life. But at the end of these seventy years,
it will happen to Tyre as in the song of the prostitute:

16"Take up a harp, walk through the city,
O prostitute forgotten;
play the harp well, sing many a song,
so that you will be remembered."

17At the end of seventy years, the LORD will deal with Tyre.
She will return to her hire as a prostitute and will ply her
trade with all the kingdoms on the face of the earth.
18Yet her profit and her earnings will be set apart for the

a 10 Or *Till your land as along the Nile,*
O city of Tarshish;
you no longer have a harbor.
(See Dead Sea Scrolls and Septuagint.)
b 11 Hebrew *Canaan*　　c 12 Hebrew *Kittim*　　d 13 That is, Babylonians

LORD; they will not be stored up or hoarded. Her profits will go to those who live before the LORD, for abundant food and fine clothes.

The LORD's Devastation of the Earth

24 See, the LORD is going to lay waste the earth
and devastate it;
he will ruin its face
and scatter its inhabitants—
²it will be the same
for priest as for people,
for master as for servant,
for mistress as for maid,
for seller as for buyer,
for borrower as for lender,
for debtor as for creditor.
³The earth will be completely laid waste
and totally plundered.

The LORD has spoken this word.

⁴The earth dries up and withers,
the world languishes and withers,
the exalted of the earth languish.
⁵The earth is defiled by its people;
they have disobeyed the laws,
violated the statutes
and broken the everlasting covenant.
⁶Therefore a curse consumes the earth;
its people must bear their guilt.
Therefore earth's inhabitants are burned up,
and very few are left.
⁷The new wine dries up and the vine withers;
all the merrymakers groan.
⁸The gay tambourines are stilled,

the noise of the revelers has stopped,
the joyful harp falls silent.
⁹No longer do they drink wine with a song;
the beer is bitter to its drinkers.
¹⁰The ruined city lies desolate;
the entrance to every house is barred.
¹¹In the streets they cry out for wine;
all joy turns to gloom,
all gaiety is banished from the earth.
¹²The city is left in ruins,
its gate is battered to pieces.
¹³So will it be in the earth
and among the nations—
as when an olive tree is beaten,
or as when gleanings are left after the grape
harvest.

¹⁴They raise their voices, they shout for joy;
from the west they acclaim the LORD's
majesty.
¹⁵Therefore in the east give glory to the LORD;
exalt the name of the LORD, the God of
Israel,
in the islands of the sea.
¹⁶From the ends of the earth we hear singing:
"Glory to the Righteous One."

But I said, "I waste away, I waste away!
Woe to me!
The treacherous betray!
With treachery the treacherous betray!"
¹⁷Terror and pit and snare await you,
O people of the earth!
¹⁸Whoever flees at the sound of terror
will fall into a pit;
whoever climbs out of the pit
will be caught in a snare.

The floodgates of the heavens are opened,
   the foundations of the earth shake.
¹⁹The earth is broken up,
   the earth is split asunder,
   the earth is thoroughly shaken.
²⁰The earth reels like a drunkard,
   it sways like a hut in the wind;
 so heavy upon it is the guilt of its rebellion
   that it falls—never to rise again.

²¹In that day the LORD will punish
   the powers in the heavens above
   and the kings on the earth below.
²²They will be herded together
   like prisoners bound in a dungeon;
 they will be shut up in prison,
   and be punished after many days.
²³The moon will be abashed, the sun ashamed;
   for the LORD Almighty will reign
 on Mount Zion and in Jerusalem,
   and before its elders, gloriously.

Praise to the LORD

25 O LORD, you are my God;
   I will exalt you and praise your name,
 for in perfect faithfulness
   you have done marvelous things,
   things planned long ago.
²You have made the city a heap of rubble,
   the fortified town a ruin,
 the stronghold of the foreigners to be a city no
      more;
   it will never be rebuilt.
³Therefore strong peoples will honor you;
   cities of ruthless nations will revere you.
⁴You have been a refuge for the poor,
   a refuge for the needy in his distress,

a shelter from the storm
and a shade from the heat:
For the breath of the ruthless
is like a storm driving against a wall
5 and like the heat of the desert.
You silence the uproar of foreigners;
as heat is reduced by the shadow of a cloud,
so the song of the ruthless is stilled.

⁶On this mountain the LORD Almighty will
prepare
a feast of rich food for all peoples,
a banquet of aged wine—
the best of meats and the finest of wines.
⁷On this mountain he will destroy
the shroud that enfolds all peoples,
the sheet that covers all nations—
8 he will swallow up death forever.
The Sovereign LORD will wipe away the tears
from all faces;
he will remove the disgrace of his people
from all the earth.
The LORD has spoken.

⁹In that day they will say,

"Surely this is our God;
we trusted in him, and he saved us.
This is the LORD, we trusted in him;
let us rejoice and be glad in his salvation."

¹⁰The hand of the LORD will rest on this mountain;
but Mo·ab will be trampled under him
as straw is trampled down in the manure.
¹¹They will spread out their hands in it,
as a swimmer spreads out his hands to swim.
God will bring down their pride

despite the cleverness[a] of their hands.
¹²He will bring down your high fortified walls
and lay them low;
he will bring them down to the ground—
to the very dust.

A Song of Praise

26 In that day this song will be sung in the land of Judah:

We have a strong city;
God makes salvation
its walls and ramparts.
²Open the gates
that the righteous nation may enter,
the nation that keeps faith.
³You will keep in perfect peace
him whose mind is steadfast,
because he trusts in you.
⁴Trust in the LORD forever,
for the LORD, the LORD, is the Rock eternal.
⁵He humbles those who dwell on high,
he lays the lofty city low;
he levels it to the ground
and casts it down to the dust.
⁶Feet trample it down—
the feet of the oppressed,
the footsteps of the poor.

⁷The path of the righteous is level;
O upright One, you make the way of the
righteous smooth.
⁸Yes, LORD, walking in the way of your laws,[b]
we wait for you;
your name and renown
are the desire of our hearts.
⁹My soul yearns for you in the night;

[a] 11 The meaning of the Hebrew word is uncertain.   [b] 8 Or *judgments*

in the morning my spirit longs for you.
When your judgments come upon the earth,
   the people of the world learn righteousness.
¹⁰Though grace is shown to the wicked,
   he does not learn righteousness;
even in a land of uprightness he goes on doing
      evil
   and regards not the majesty of the LORD.
¹¹O LORD, your hand is lifted high,
   but they do not see it.
Let them see your zeal for your people and be
      put to shame;
   let the fire reserved for your enemies consume
      them.

¹²LORD, you establish peace for us;
   all that we have accomplished you have done
      for us.
¹³O LORD, our God, other lords besides you have
      ruled over us,
   but your name alone do we honor.
¹⁴They are now dead, they live no more;
   those departed spirits do not rise.
You punished them and brought them to ruin;
   you wiped out all memory of them.
¹⁵You have enlarged the nation, O LORD;
   you have enlarged the nation.
You have gained honor for yourself;
   you have extended all the borders of the land.

¹⁶LORD, they came to you in their distress;
   when you disciplined them,
   they could barely whisper a prayer.ᵃ
¹⁷As a woman with child and about to give birth
   writhes and cries out in her pain,

ᵃ 16 The meaning of the Hebrew clause is uncertain.

so were we in your presence, O LORD.
¹⁸We were with child, we writhed in pain,
but we gave birth to wind.
We have not brought salvation to the earth;
we have not given birth to people of the
world.

¹⁹But your dead will live,
their bodies will rise.
You who dwell in the dust,
wake up and shout for joy!
Your dew is like the dew of the morning;
the earth will give birth to the dead.

²⁰Go, my people, enter your rooms
and shut the doors behind you;
hide yourselves for a little while
until his wrath has passed by.
²¹See, the LORD is coming out of his dwelling
to punish the people of the earth for their sins.
The earth will disclose the blood shed upon her;
she will conceal her slain no longer.

Deliverance of Israel

27 In that day,
the LORD will punish with his sword,
his fierce, great and powerful sword,
Leviathan the gliding serpent,
Leviathan the coiling serpent;
he will slay the monster of the sea.

²In that day—
"Sing about a fruitful vineyard:
³ I, the LORD, watch over it;
I water it continually.
I guard it day and night
so that no one may harm it.

⁴ I am not angry.
If only there were briers and thorns confronting
      me!
   I would march against them in battle;
   I would set them all on fire.
⁵Or else let them come to me for refuge;
   let them make peace with me,
   yes, let them make peace with me."

⁶In days to come Jacob will take root,
   Israel will bud and blossom
   and fill all the world with fruit.

⁷Has ⸢the Lord⸣ struck her
   as he struck down those who struck her?
 Has she been killed
   as those were killed who killed her?
⁸By warfare*a* and exile you contend with her—
   with his fierce blast he drives her out,
   as on a day the east wind blows.
⁹By this, then, will Jacob's guilt be atoned for,
   and this will be the full fruitage of the removal
      of his sin:
 When he makes all the altar stones
   to be like chalk stones crushed to pieces,
 no Asherah poles or incense altars
   will be left standing.
¹⁰The fortified city stands desolate,
   an abandoned settlement, forsaken like the
      desert;
 there the calves graze,
   there they lie down;
   they strip its branches bare.
¹¹When its twigs are dry, they are broken off,
   and women come and make fires with them.
 For this is a people without understanding;

a 8 See Septuagint; the meaning of the Hebrew word is uncertain.

so their Maker has no compassion on them,
and their Creator shows them no favor.

¹²In that day the LORD will thresh from the flowing Euphrates^a to the Wadi of Egypt, and you, O Israelites, will be gathered up one by one. ¹³And in that day a great trumpet will sound. Those who were perishing in Assyria and those who were exiled in Egypt will come and worship the LORD on the holy mountain in Jerusalem.

Woe to Ephra·im

28 Woe to that wreath, the pride of Ephra·im's
drunkards,
to the fading flower, his glorious beauty,
set on the head of a fertile valley—
to that city, the pride of those laid low by
wine!
²See, the Lord has one who is powerful and
strong.
Like a hailstorm and a destructive wind,
like a driving rain and a flooding downpour,
he will throw it forcefully to the ground.
³That wreath, the pride of Ephra·im's drunkards,
will be trampled underfoot.
⁴That fading flower, his glorious beauty,
set on the head of a fertile valley,
will be like a fig ripe before harvest—
as soon as someone sees it and takes it in his
hand,
he gulps it down.

⁵In that day the LORD Almighty
will be a glorious crown,

_a_ 12 Hebrew _the flowing River_

   a beautiful wreath
     for the remnant of his people.
⁶He will be a spirit of justice
     to him who sits in judgment,
   a source of strength
     to those who turn back the battle at the gate.

⁷And these also stagger from wine
     and reel from beer:
Priests and prophets stagger from beer
     and are befuddled with wine;
they reel from beer,
     they stagger in seeing their visions,
     they stumble in rendering decisions.
⁸All the tables are covered with vomit,
     and there is not a spot without filth.

⁹"Who is it he is trying to teach?
     To whom is he explaining his message?
To children weaned from their milk,
     to those just taken from the breast?
¹⁰For it is:
     ᵃDo and do, do and do,
     rule on rule, rule on rule;ᵃ
     a little here, a little there."

¹¹Very well then, with foreign lips and strange
     tongues
   God will speak to this people,
¹²to whom he said,
     "This is the resting place, let the weary rest";
and, "This is the place of repose"—
     but they would not listen.

ᵃ⁻ᵃ 10 Hebrew *sav lasav sav lasav kav lakav kav lakav* (possibly meaningless sounds; perhaps a mimicking of the prophet's words)

¹³So then, the word of the LORD to them will
become:
^aDo and do, do and do,
rule on rule, rule on rule;^a
a little here, a little there—
so that they will go and fall backward,
be injured and snared and captured.

¹⁴Therefore hear the word of the LORD, you
scoffers,
who rule this people in Jerusalem.
¹⁵You boast, "We have entered into a covenant
with death,
with the grave^b we have made an agreement.
When an overwhelming scourge sweeps by,
it cannot touch us,
for we have made a lie our refuge
and false gods our hiding place."

¹⁶So this is what the Sovereign LORD says:

See, I lay a stone in Zion,
a tested stone,
a precious cornerstone for a sure foundation;
the one who trusts will never be dismayed.
¹⁷I will make justice the measuring line
and righteousness the plumb line;
hail will sweep away your refuge, the lie,
and water will overflow your hiding place.
¹⁸Your covenant with death will be annulled;
your agreement with the grave^b will not stand.
When the overwhelming scourge sweeps by,
you will be beaten down by it.
¹⁹As often as it comes it will carry you away;

---

^{a-a}13 Hebrew *sav lasav sav lasav kav lakav kav lakav* (possibly meaningless sounds;
perhaps a mimicking of the prophet's words)   ^b15,18 Hebrew *Sheol*

morning after morning, by day and by night,
it will sweep through.
The understanding of this message
will bring sheer terror.
20The bed is too short to stretch out on,
the blanket too narrow to wrap around you.
21The LORD will rise up as he did at Mount Perazim,
he will rouse himself as in the valley of
Gibeon—
to do his work, his strange work,
and perform his task, his alien task.
22Now stop your scoffing,
or your chains will become heavier;
the Lord, the LORD Almighty, has told me
of the destruction decreed against the whole
land.

23Listen and hear my voice;
pay attention and hear what I say!
24When a farmer plows for planting, does he plow
continually?
Does he keep on breaking up and harrowing
the soil?
25When he has leveled the surface,
does he not sow caraway and scatter cummin?
Does he not plant wheat in its place,a
barley in its plot,a
and rye in its field?
26His God instructs him
and teaches him the ways of the farmer.

27Caraway is not threshed with a sledge,
nor is a cartwheel rolled over cummin;
caraway is beaten out with a rod,

a 25 The meaning of the Hebrew word is uncertain.

and cummin with a stick.
²⁸Grain must be ground to make bread;
    so one does not go on threshing it forever.
Though he drives the wheels of his threshing
    cart over it,
    his horses do not grind it.
²⁹All this also comes from the Lord Almighty,
    wonderful in counsel and magnificent in
    wisdom.

Woe to David's City

29 Woe to you, Ari·el, Ari·el,
    the city where David settled!
Add year to year
    and let your cycle of festivals go on.
²Yet I will besiege Ari·el;
    she will mourn and lament,
    she will be to me like an altar hearth.ᵃ
³I will encamp against you all around;
    I will encircle you with towers
    and set up my siege works against you.
⁴Brought low, you will speak from the ground;
    your speech will mumble out of the dust.
Your voice will come ghostlike from the earth;
    out of the dust your speech will whisper.

⁵But your many enemies will become like fine
    dust,
    the ruthless hordes like blown chaff.
Suddenly, in an instant,
⁶   the Lord Almighty will come
with thunder and earthquake and great noise,
    with windstorm and tempest and flames of a
    devouring fire.

ᵃ 2 Hebrew *like ariel*

⁷Then the hordes of all the nations that fight
   against Ari·el,
   that attack her and her fortress, and besiege
      her,
will be as it is with a dream,
   with a vision in the night—
⁸as when a hungry man dreams that he is
      eating,
   but he awakens, and his hunger remains;
as when a thirsty man dreams that he is
      drinking,
   but he awakens faint, with his thirst
      unquenched.
So will it be with the hordes of all the nations
   that fight against Mount Zion.

⁹Be stunned and amazed,
   blind yourselves and be sightless;
be drunk, but not from wine,
   stagger, but not from beer.
¹⁰The Lord has brought over you a deep sleep:
   He has sealed your eyes—the prophets;
   he has covered your heads—the seers.

¹¹For you this whole vision is nothing but words sealed in
a scroll. And if you give the scroll to someone who can read,
and say to him, "Read this, please," he will answer, "I can't;
it is sealed." ¹²Or if you give the scroll to someone who
cannot read, and say, "Read this, please," he will answer, "I
don't know how to read."

¹³The Lord says:

   "These people come near to me with their mouth
      and honor me with their lips,
   but their hearts are far from me.
   Their worship of me

is made up only of rules taught by men.*a*

14Therefore once more I will astound these people
with wonder upon wonder;
the wisdom of the wise will perish,
the intelligence of the intelligent will vanish."
15Woe to those who go to great depths
to hide their plans from the LORD,
who do their work in darkness and think,
"Who sees us? Who will know?"
16You turn things upside down,
as if the potter were thought to be like the
clay!
Shall what is formed say to him who formed it,
"He did not make me"?
Can the pot say of the potter,
"He knows nothing"?

17In a very short time, will not Lebanon be turned
into a fertile field
and the fertile field seem like a forest?
18In that day the deaf will hear the words of the
scroll,
and out of gloom and darkness
the eyes of the blind will see.
19Once more the humble will rejoice in the LORD;
the needy will rejoice in the Holy One of
Israel.
20The ruthless will vanish,
the scoffer will disappear,
and all who have an eye for evil will be cut
down—
21those who with a word make a man out to be
guilty,
who ensnare the defender in court

---

a 13 Hebrew; Septuagint *they worship me in vain,*
their teachings are but rules made by men.

and with false testimony deprive the innocent
   of justice.

²²Therefore this is what the LORD, who redeemed
Abraham, says to the house of Jacob:

"No longer will Jacob be ashamed;
   no longer will their faces grow pale.
²³When they see among them their children,
   the work of my hands,
   they will keep my name holy;
they will acknowledge the holiness of the Holy
   One of Jacob,
   and will stand in awe of the God of Israel.
²⁴Those who are wayward in spirit will gain
   understanding;
   those who complain will accept instruction."

Woe to the Obstinate Nation

30 "Woe to the obstinate children,"
   declares the LORD,
"to those who carry out plans that are not mine,
   forming an alliance, but not by my Spirit,
   heaping sin upon sin;
²who go down to Egypt
   without consulting me;
who look for help to the Pharaoh's protection,
   to Egypt's shade for refuge.
³But the Pharaoh's protection will be to your
   shame,
   Egypt's shade will bring you disgrace.
⁴Though they have officials in Zo·an,
   and their envoys have arrived in Hanes,
⁵everyone will be put to shame
   because of a people useless to them,
who bring neither help nor advantage,
   but only shame and disgrace."

⁶An oracle concerning the animals of the Negev:

Through a land of hardship and distress,
of lions and lionesses,
of adders and darting snakes,
the envoys carry their riches on donkeys' backs,
their treasures on the humps of camels,
to that unprofitable nation,
⁷   to Egypt, whose help is utterly useless.
Therefore I call her
Rahab the Do-Nothing.

⁸Go now, write it on a tablet for them,
inscribe it on a scroll,
that for the days to come
it may be an everlasting witness.
⁹These are rebellious people, deceitful children,
children unwilling to listen to the LORD's
instruction.
¹⁰They say to the seers,
"See no more visions!"
and to the prophets,
"Give us no more visions of what is right!
Tell us pleasant things,
prophesy illusions.
¹¹Leave this way,
get off this path,
and stop confronting us
with the Holy One of Israel!"

¹²Therefore, this is what the Holy One of Israel says:

"Because you have rejected this message,
relied on oppression,
and depended on deceit,
¹³this sin will become for you
like a high wall, cracked and bulging,
that collapses suddenly, in an instant.

¹⁴It will break in pieces like pottery,
　　shattered so mercilessly
　that among its pieces not a fragment will be
　　　found
　　　for taking coals from a hearth
　　　or scooping water out of a cistern."

¹⁵This is what the Sovereign LORD, the Holy One of Israel, says:

　　"In repentance and rest is your salvation,
　　　in quietness and trust is your strength,
　　　but you would have none of it.
¹⁶You said, 'No, we will flee on horses.'
　　Therefore you will flee!
　You said, 'We will ride off on swift horses.'
　　Therefore your pursuers will be swift!
¹⁷A thousand will flee
　　at the threat of one;
　at the threat of five
　　you will all flee away,
　till you are left
　　like a flagstaff on a mountaintop,
　　like a banner on a hill."

¹⁸Yet the LORD longs to be gracious to you;
　　he rises to show you compassion.
　For the LORD is a God of justice.
　　Blessed are all who wait for him!

¹⁹O people of Zion, who live in Jerusalem, you will weep no more. How gracious he will be when you cry for help! As soon as he hears, he will answer you. ²⁰Although the Lord gives you the bread of adversity and the water of affliction, your teachers will be hidden no more; with your own eyes you will see them. ²¹Whether you turn to the right or to the left, your ears will hear a voice behind you, saying, "This is the way; walk in it." ²²Then you will defile your idols overlaid

with silver and your images covered with gold; you will throw them away like a menstrual cloth and say to them, "Away with you!"

²³He will also send you rain for the seed you sow in the ground, and the food that comes from the land will be rich and plentiful. In that day your cattle will graze in broad meadows. ²⁴The oxen and donkeys that work the soil will eat fodder and mash, spread out with fork and shovel. ²⁵In the day of great slaughter, when the towers fall, streams of water will flow on every high mountain and every lofty hill. ²⁶The moon will shine like the sun, and the sunlight will be seven times brighter, like the light of seven full days, when the LORD binds up the bruises of his people and heals the wounds he inflicted.

²⁷See, the Name of the LORD comes from afar,
    with burning anger and dense clouds of
        smoke;
  his lips are full of wrath,
    and his tongue is a consuming fire.
²⁸His breath is like a rushing torrent,
    rising up to the neck.
He shakes the nations in the sieve of destruction;
    he places in the jaws of the peoples
    a bit that leads them astray.
²⁹And you will sing
    as on the night you celebrate a holy festival;
  your hearts will rejoice
    as when people go up with flutes
  to the mountain of the LORD,
    to the Rock of Israel.
³⁰The LORD will cause men to hear his majestic
        voice
    and will make them see his arm coming down,
  with raging anger and consuming fire,
    with cloudburst, thunderstorm and hail.

³¹The voice of the LORD will shatter Assyria;
  with his scepter he will strike them down.
³²Every stroke the LORD lays on them
  with his punishing rod
will be to the music of tambourines and harps,
  as he fights them in battle with the blows of
    his arm.
³³Topheth has long been prepared;
  ·it has been made ready for the king.
Its fire pit has been made deep and wide,
  with an abundance of fire and wood;
the breath of the LORD,
  like a stream of burning sulfur,
  sets it ablaze.

Woe to Those Who Rely on Egypt

31 Woe to those who go down to Egypt for help,
    who rely on horses,
  who trust in the multitude of their chariots
    and in the great strength of their horsemen,
  but do not look to the Holy One of Israel,
    or seek help from the LORD.
²Yet he too is wise and can bring disaster;
  he does not take back his words.
He will rise up against the house of the wicked,
  against those who help evildoers.
³But the Egyptians are men and not God;
  their horses are flesh and not spirit.
When the LORD stretches out his hand,
  he who helps will stumble,
  he who is helped will fall;
  both will perish together.

⁴For this is what the LORD says to me:

  "As a lion growls,
    a great lion over his prey—
  and though a whole band of shepherds

is called together against him,
he is not frightened by their shouts,
or disturbed by their clamor—
so the LORD Almighty will come down
to do battle on Mount Zion and on its heights.
⁵Like birds hovering overhead,
the LORD Almighty will shield Jerusalem;
he will shield and deliver it,
he will 'pass over' it and will rescue it."

⁶Return to him you have so greatly revolted against, O
Israelites. ⁷For in that day every one of you will reject the
idols of silver and gold your sinful hands have made.

⁸"Assyria will fall by a sword that is not of man;
a sword, not of mortals, will devour them.
They will flee before the sword,
and their young men will be put to forced
labor.
⁹Their stronghold will fall because of terror;
at sight of the battle standard their
commanders will panic,"
declares the LORD,
whose fire is in Zion,
whose furnace is in Jerusalem.

The Kingdom of Righteousness

32 See, a king will reign in righteousness,
and rulers will rule with justice.
²He will be like a shelter from the wind,
or a refuge from the storm,
like streams of water in the desert,
or the shadow of a great rock in a thirsty land.

³Then the eyes of those who see will no longer be
closed,
and the ears of those who hear will listen.
⁴The mind of the rash will know and understand,

and the stammering tongue will be fluent and
  clear.
⁵No longer will the fool be called noble,
  nor the scoundrel be highly respected.
⁶For the fool speaks folly,
  his mind is busy with evil:
He practices ungodliness
  and spreads error concerning the LORD;
the hungry he leaves empty
  and from the thirsty he withholds water.
⁷The scoundrel's methods are wicked,
  he makes up evil schemes
to destroy the poor with lies,
  even when the plea of the needy is just.
⁸But the noble man makes noble plans,
  and by noble deeds he stands.

The Women of Jerusalem

⁹You women who are so complacent,
  rise up and listen to me;
you daughters who feel secure,
  hear what I have to say!
¹⁰In little more than a year
  you who feel secure will tremble;
the grape harvest will fail,
  and the harvest of fruit will not come.
¹¹Tremble, you complacent women;
  shudder, you daughters who feel secure!
Strip off your clothes,
  put sackcloth around your waists.
¹²Beat your breasts for the pleasant fields,
  for the fruitful vines
¹³and for the land of my people,
  a land overgrown with thorns and briers—
yes, mourn for all houses of merriment
  and for this city of revelry.

¹⁴The palace will be abandoned,
    the noisy city deserted;
  citadel and watchtower will become a wasteland
      forever,
    the delight of donkeys, a pasture for flocks,
¹⁵till the Spirit is poured upon us from on high,
    and the desert becomes a fertile field,
    and the fertile field seems like a forest.
¹⁶Justice will dwell in the desert,
    and righteousness live in the fertile field.
¹⁷The fruit of righteousness will be peace;
    the effect of righteousness will be quietness
      and confidence forever.
¹⁸My people will live in peaceful dwelling places,
    in secure homes,
    in undisturbed places of rest.
¹⁹Though hail flattens the forest,
    and the city is leveled completely,
²⁰how blessed you will be,
    sowing your seed by every stream,
    and letting your oxen and donkeys range free.

Distress and Help

33 Woe to you, O destroyer,
    you who have not been destroyed!
Woe to you, O traitor,
    you who have not been betrayed!
When you stop destroying,
    you will be destroyed;
when you stop betraying,
    you will be betrayed.

²O LORD, be gracious to us;
    we long for you.
Be our strength every morning,
    our salvation in time of distress.

³At the thunder of your voice, the peoples flee;
when you rise up, the nations scatter.
⁴Your plunder, O nations, is harvested as by
young locusts;
like a swarm of locusts men pounce on it.

⁵The LORD is exalted, for he dwells on high;
he will fill Zion with justice and righteousness.
⁶He will be the sure foundation for your times,
a rich store of salvation and wisdom and
knowledge;
the fear of the LORD is the key to this
treasure.ᵃ

⁷Look, their brave men cry aloud in the streets;
the envoys of peace weep bitterly.
⁸The highways are deserted,
no travelers are on the roads.
The treaty is broken,
its witnessesᵇ are despised,
no one is respected.
⁹The land mourns and wastes away,
Lebanon is ashamed and withers;
Sharon is like the Arabah,
and Bashan and Carmel drop their leaves.

¹⁰"Now I will arise," says the LORD.
"Now will I be exalted;
now will I be lifted up.
¹¹You conceive chaff,
you give birth to straw;
your breath is a fire that consumes you.
¹²The peoples will be burned as if to lime;
like cut thornbushes they will be set ablaze."

ᵃ6 Or *is a treasure from him.*   ᵇ8 Dead Sea Scrolls; Masoretic Text *the cities*

¹³You who are far away, hear what I have done;
    you who are near, acknowledge my power!
¹⁴The sinners in Zion are terrified;
    trembling grips the godless:
  "Who of us can dwell with the consuming fire?
  Who of us can dwell with everlasting
        burning?"
¹⁵He who lives righteously
    and speaks what is right,
  who rejects gain from extortion
    and keeps his hand from accepting bribes,
  who stops his ears against plots of murder
    and shuts his eyes against contemplating evil—
¹⁶this is the man who will dwell on the heights,
    whose refuge will be the mountain fortress.
  His bread will be supplied,
    and water will not fail him.

¹⁷Your eyes will see the king in his beauty
    and view a land that stretches afar.
¹⁸In your thoughts you will ponder the former
        terror:
  "Where is that chief officer?
  Where is the one who took the revenue?
  Where is the officer in charge of the towers?"
¹⁹You will see those arrogant people no more,
    those people of an obscure speech,
    with their strange, incomprehensible tongue.

²⁰Look upon Zion, the city of our festivals;
    your eyes will see Jerusalem,
    a peaceful abode, a tent that will not be moved;
  its stakes will never be pulled up,
    nor any of its ropes broken.
²¹There the LORD will be our Mighty One.
    It will be like a place of broad rivers and
        streams.

No galley with its oars will ride them,
 no mighty ship will sail them.
22For the LORD is our judge;
 the LORD is our lawgiver;
 the LORD is our king,
  it is he who will save us.

23Your rigging hangs loose:
 The mast is not held secure,
 the sail is not spread.
Then an abundance of spoils will be divided
 and even the lame will carry off plunder.
24No one living in Zion will say, "I am ill,"
 and the sins of those who dwell there will be
  forgiven.

Judgment Against the Nations

34 Come near, you nations, and listen;
 pay attention, you peoples!
Let the earth hear, and all that is in it,
 the world, and all that comes out of it!
2The LORD is angry with all nations;
 his wrath is upon all their armies.
He will totally destroy*a* them,
 he will give them over to slaughter.
3Their slain will be thrown out,
 their dead bodies will send up a stench;
 the mountains will be soaked with their
  blood.
4All the stars of the heavens will be dissolved,
 and the sky rolled up like a scroll;
all the starry host will fall
 like withered leaves from the vine,
 like shriveled figs from the fig tree.

---

*a 2 The Hebrew term refers to the practice of devoting things or persons irrevocably
to the LORD, often by total destruction.

⁵My sword has drunk its fill in the heavens;
  see, it descends in judgment on Edom,
  the people I have totally destroyed.ᵃ
⁶The sword of the LORD is bathed in blood,
  it is covered with fat—
the blood of lambs and goats,
  fat from the kidneys of rams.
For the LORD has a sacrifice in Bozrah
  and a great slaughter in Edom.
⁷And the wild oxen will fall with them,
  the bull calves and the great bulls.
Their land will be drenched with blood,
  and the dust will be soaked with fat.

⁸For the LORD has a day of vengeance,
  a year of retribution, to uphold Zion's cause.
⁹Edom's streams will be turned into pitch,
  her dust into burning sulfur;
  her land will become blazing pitch!
¹⁰It will not be quenched night and day;
  its smoke will rise forever.
From generation to generation it will lie desolate;
  no one will ever pass through it again.
¹¹The desert owlᵇ and screech owlᵇ will possess it;
  the great owlᵇ and the raven will nest there.
God will stretch out over Edom
  the measuring line of chaos
  and the plumb line of desolation.
¹²Her nobles will have nothing there to be called a
      kingdom,
  all her princes will vanish away.
¹³Thorns will overrun her citadels,
  nettles and brambles her strongholds.

ᵃ 5 The Hebrew term refers to the practice of devoting things or persons irrevocably
to the LORD, often by total destruction.   ᵇ 11 The precise identification of these
birds is uncertain.

> She will become a haunt for jackals,
>> a home for ostriches.
> ¹⁴Desert creatures will meet with hyenas,
>> and goats will bleat to each other;
> there the night creatures will also repose
>> and find for themselves places of rest.
> ¹⁵The owl will nest there and lay eggs,
>> she will hatch them, and care for her young
>>> under her wings;
> there also the falcons will gather,
>> each with her mate.

¹⁶Look in the scroll of the LORD and read:

> None of these will be missing,
>> not one will lack her mate.
> For it is his mouth that has given the order,
>> and his Spirit will gather them together.
> ¹⁷He allots their portions;
>> his hand distributes them by measure.
> They will possess it forever
>> and dwell there from generation to
>>> generation.

Joy of the Redeemed

35 The desert and the parched land will be glad;
> the wilderness will rejoice and blossom.
> Like the crocus, ²it will burst into bloom;
>> it will rejoice greatly and shout for joy.
> The glory of Lebanon will be given to it,
>> the splendor of Carmel and Sharon;
> they will see the glory of the LORD,
>> the splendor of our God.

> ³Strengthen the feeble hands,
>> steady the knees that give way;
> ⁴say to those with fearful hearts,

"Be strong, do not fear;
your God will come,
   he will come with vengeance;
with divine retribution
   he will come to save you."

⁵Then will the eyes of the blind be opened
   and the ears of the deaf unstopped.
⁶Then will the lame leap like a deer,
   and the tongue of the dumb shout for joy.
Water will gush forth in the wilderness
   and streams in the desert.
⁷The burning sand will become a pool,
   the thirsty ground bubbling springs.
In the haunts where jackals once lay,
   grass and reeds and papyrus will grow.

⁸And a highway will be there;
   it will be called The Way of Holiness.
The unclean will not journey on it.
   It will be for those who walk in that
     Way;
   wicked fools will not go about on it.*a*
⁹No lion will be there,
   nor will any ferocious beast get up on it;
   they will not be found there.
But only the redeemed will walk there,
¹⁰ and the ransomed of the LORD will
     return.
They will enter Zion with singing;
   everlasting joy will crown their heads.
Gladness and joy will overtake them,
   and sorrow and sighing will flee away.

a 8 Or the simple will not stray from it.

Sennacherib Threatens Jerusalem

36 In the fourteenth year of King Hezekiah's reign, Sennacherib king of Assyria attacked all the fortified cities of Judah and captured them. ²Then the king of Assyria sent his field commander with a large army from Lachish to King Hezekiah at Jerusalem. When the commander stopped at the aqueduct of the Upper Pool, on the road to the Washerman's Field, ³Eliakim son of Hilkiah the palace administrator, Shebna the secretary, and Joah son of Asaph the recorder went out to him.

⁴The field commander said to them, "Tell Hezekiah, 'This is what the great king, the king of Assyria, says: On what are you basing this confidence of yours? ⁵You say you have strategy and military strength—but you speak only empty words. On whom are you depending, that you rebel against me? ⁶Look now, you are depending on Egypt, that splintered reed of a staff, which pierces a man's hand and wounds him if he leans on it! Such is the Pharaoh, the king of Egypt, to all who depend on him. ⁷And if you say to me, "We are depending on the LORD our God"—isn't he the one whose high places and altars Hezekiah removed, saying to Judah and Jerusalem, "You must worship before this altar"?

⁸" 'Come now, make a bargain with my master, the king of Assyria: I will give you two thousand horses, if you can put riders on them. ⁹How then can you repulse one officer of the least of my master's officials, even though you are depending on Egypt for chariots and horsemen? ¹⁰Furthermore, have I come to attack and destroy this land without the LORD? The LORD himself told me to march against this country and destroy it.' "

¹¹Then Eliakim, Shebna and Joah said to the field commander, "Please speak to your servants in Aramaic, since we understand it. Don't speak to us in Hebrew in the hearing of the people on the wall."

¹²But the commander replied, "Was it only to your master and you that my master sent me to say these things, and not

to the men sitting on the wall—who, like you, will have to eat their own filth and drink their own urine?"

¹³Then the commander stood and shouted in Hebrew, "Hear the words of the great king, the king of Assyria! ¹⁴This is what the king says: Do not let Hezekiah deceive you. He cannot deliver you! ¹⁵Do not let Hezekiah persuade you to trust in the LORD when he says 'The LORD will surely deliver us; this city will not be given into the hand of the king of Assyria.'

¹⁶"Do not listen to Hezekiah. This is what the king of Assyria says: Make peace with me and come out to me. Then every one of you will eat from his own vine and fig tree and drink water from his own cistern, ¹⁷until I come and take you to a land like your own—a land of grain and new wine, a land of bread and vineyards.

¹⁸"Do not let Hezekiah mislead you when he says, 'The LORD will deliver us.' Has the god of any nation ever delivered his land from the hand of the king of Assyria? ¹⁹Where are the gods of Hamath and Arpad? Where are the gods of Sepharva·im? Have they rescued Samaria from my hand? ²⁰Who of all the gods of these countries has been able to save his land from me? So how can the LORD deliver Jerusalem from my hand?"

²¹But the people remained silent and said nothing in reply, because the king had commanded, "Do not answer him."

²²Then Eliakim son of Hilkiah the palace administrator, Shebna the secretary, and Joah son of Asaph the recorder went to Hezekiah, with their clothes torn, and told him what the field commander had said.

Jerusalem's Deliverance Foretold

37 When King Hezekiah heard this, he tore his clothes and put on sackcloth and went into the temple of the LORD. ²He sent Eliakim the palace administrator, Shebna the secretary, and the leading priests, all wearing sackcloth, to the prophet Isaiah son of Amoz. ³They told him, "This is what Hezekiah says: This day is a day of distress and rebuke and disgrace, as when children come to the point of birth and there is no strength to deliver them. [4]It may be that the LORD your God will hear the words of the field commander, whom his master, the king of Assyria, has sent to ridicule the living God, and that he will rebuke him for the words the LORD your God has heard. Therefore pray for the remnant that still survives."

[5]When King Hezekiah's officials came to Isaiah, [6]Isaiah said to them, "Tell your master, 'This is what the LORD says: Do not be afraid of what you have heard—those words with which the underlings of the king of Assyria have blasphemed me. [7]Listen! I am going to put such a spirit in him that when he hears a certain report, he will return to his own country, and there I will have him cut down with the sword.' "

[8]When the field commander heard that the king of Assyria had left Lachish, he withdrew and found the king fighting against Libnah.

[9]Now Sennacherib received a report that Tirhakah, the Cushite[a] king ˌof Egyptˌ, was marching out to fight against him. So when he heard it, he sent messengers to Hezekiah with this word: [10]"Say to Hezekiah king of Judah: Do not let the god you depend on deceive you when he says, 'Jerusalem will not be handed over to the king of Assyria.' [11]Surely you have heard what the kings of Assyria have done to all the countries, destroying them completely. And will you be delivered? [12]Did the gods of the nations that were destroyed by my forefathers deliver them—the gods of Gozan, Haran, Rezeph and the people of Eden who were in Tel Assar? [13]Where is the king of Hamath, the king of Arpad, the king of the city of Sepharva·im, or of Hena or Ivvah?"

Hezekiah's Prayer

[14]Hezekiah received the letter from the messengers and read it. Then he went up to the temple of the LORD and spread

[a] 9 That is, from ancient Ethiopia

it out before the LORD. ¹⁵And Hezekiah prayed to the LORD: ¹⁶"O LORD Almighty, God of Israel, enthroned between the cherubim, you alone are God over all the kingdoms of the earth. You have made heaven and earth. ¹⁷Give ear, O LORD, and hear; open your eyes, O LORD, and see; listen to all the words Sennacherib has sent to insult the living God.

¹⁸"It is true, O LORD, that the Assyrian kings have laid waste all these peoples and their lands. ¹⁹They have thrown their gods into the fire and destroyed them, for they were not gods but only wood and stone, fashioned by human hands. ²⁰Now, O LORD our God, deliver us from his hand, so that all kingdoms on earth may know that you alone, O LORD, are God.^a"

Sennacherib's Fall

²¹Then Isaiah son of Amoz sent a message to Hezekiah: "This is what the LORD, the God of Israel, says: Because you have prayed to me concerning Sennacherib king of Assyria, ²²this is the word the LORD has spoken against him:

The Virgin Daughter of Zion
   despises and mocks you.
The Daughter of Jerusalem
   tosses her head as you flee.
²³Who is it you have insulted and blasphemed?
   Against whom have you raised your voice
and lifted your eyes in pride?
   Against the Holy One of Israel!
²⁴By your messengers
   you have heaped insults on the Lord.
And you have said,
   'With my many chariots
I have ascended the heights of the mountains,
   the utmost heights of Lebanon.
I have cut down its tallest cedars,
   the choicest of its pines.

_a 20_ Dead Sea Scrolls (see 2 Kings 19:19); Masoretic Text _alone are the_ LORD.

I have reached its remotest heights,
    the finest of its forests.
25I have dug wells in foreign lands*a*
    and drunk the water there.
With the soles of my feet
    I have dried up all the streams of Egypt.'

26"Have you not heard?
    Long ago I ordained it.
In days of old I planned it;
    now I have brought it to pass,
so that you have turned fortified cities
    into piles of stone.
27Their people, drained of power,
    are dismayed and put to shame.
They are like plants in the field,
    like tender green shoots,
like grass sprouting on the housetops,
    scorched*b* before it grows up.

28"But I know where you stay
    and when you come and go
    and how you rage against me.
29Because you rage against me
    and because your insolence has reached my
        ears,
I will put my hook in your nose
    and my bit in your mouth,
and I will make you return
    by the way you came.

30"This will be the sign for you, O Hezekiah:

This year you will eat what grows by itself,
    and the second year what springs from that.

a 25 Dead Sea Scrolls (see 2 Kings 19:24); Masoretic Text omits *in foreign lands.*
b 27 Dead Sea Scrolls and some manuscripts of the Masoretic Text (see 2 Kings 19:26); most manuscripts of the Masoretic Text *housetops and terraced fields*

But in the third year sow and reap,
   plant vineyards and eat their fruit.
³¹Once more a remnant of the house of Judah
   will take root below and bear fruit above.
³²For out of Jerusalem will come a remnant,
   and out of Mount Zion a band of survivors.
The zeal of the LORD Almighty
   will accomplish this.

³³"Therefore this is what the LORD says concerning the king of Assyria:

He will not enter this city
   or shoot an arrow here.
He will not come before it with shield
   or build a siege ramp against it.
³⁴By the way that he came he will return;
   he will not enter this city,
                                    declares the LORD.
³⁵I will defend this city and save it,
   for my sake and for the sake of David my
      servant!"

³⁶Then the angel of the LORD went out and put to death 185,000 men in the Assyrian camp. When the people got up the next morning—there were all the dead bodies! ³⁷So Sennacherib king of Assyria broke camp and withdrew. He returned to Nineveh and stayed there.

³⁸One day, while he was worshiping in the temple of his god Nisroch, his sons Adrammelech and Sharezer cut him down with the sword, and they escaped to the land of Ararat. And Esarhaddon his son succeeded him as king.

Hezekiah's Illness

38 In those days Hezekiah became ill and was at the point of death. The prophet Isaiah son of Amoz went to him and said, "This is what the LORD says: Put your house in order, because you will die; you will not recover."

²Hezekiah turned his face to the wall and prayed to the LORD, ³"Remember, O LORD, how I have walked before you faithfully and with wholehearted devotion and have done what is good in your eyes." And Hezekiah wept bitterly.

⁴Then the word of the LORD came to Isaiah: ⁵"Go and tell Hezekiah, 'This is what the LORD, the God of your father David, says: I have heard your prayer and seen your tears; I will add fifteen years to your life. ⁶And I will deliver you and this city from the hand of the king of Assyria. I will defend this city.

⁷" 'This is the LORD's sign to you that the LORD will do what he has promised: ⁸I will make the shadow cast by the sun go back the ten steps it has gone down on the stairway of Ahaz.' " So the sunlight went back the ten steps it had gone down.

⁹A writing of Hezekiah king of Judah after his illness and recovery:

¹⁰I said, "In the prime of my life
      must I go through the gates of death^a
      and be robbed of the rest of my years?"
¹¹I said, "I will not again see the LORD,
      the LORD, in the land of the living;
   no longer will I look on mankind,
      or be with those who now dwell in this world.
¹²Like a shepherd's tent my house
      has been pulled down and taken from me.
   Like a weaver I have rolled up my life,
      and he has cut me off from the loom;
      day and night you made an end of me.
¹³I waited patiently till dawn,
      but like a lion he broke all my bones;
      day and night you made an end of me.
¹⁴I cried like a swallow or thrush,
      I moaned like a mourning dove.

^a 10 Hebrew *Sheol*

My eyes grew weak as I looked to the heavens.
I am troubled; O Lord, come to my aid!"

¹⁵But what can I say?
He has spoken to me, and he himself has done
this.
I will walk humbly all my years
because of this anguish of my soul.
¹⁶Lord, by such experiences men live;
and my spirit finds life in them too.
You restore me to health
and let me live.
¹⁷Surely it was for my benefit
that I suffered such anguish.
In your love you kept me
from the pit of destruction;
you have put all my sins
behind your back.
¹⁸For the grave^a cannot praise you,
death cannot sing your praise;
those who go down to the pit
cannot hope for your faithfulness.
¹⁹The living, the living, they praise you,
as I am doing today;
fathers tell their children
about your faithfulness.

²⁰The Lord will save me,
and we will sing with stringed instruments
all the days of our lives
in the temple of the Lord.

²¹Then Isaiah said, "Prepare a poultice of figs and apply it
to the boil, and he will recover."
²²Hezekiah had asked, "What will be the sign that I will
go up to the temple of the Lord?"

^a 18 Hebrew *Sheol*

Envoys From Babylon

39 At that time Merodach-Baladan son of Baladan king of Babylon sent Hezekiah letters and a gift, because he had heard of his illness and recovery. ²Hezekiah received the envoys gladly and showed them what was in his storehouses —the silver, the gold, the spices, the fine oil, his entire armory and everything found among his treasures. There was nothing in his palace or in all his kingdom that Hezekiah did not show them.

³Then Isaiah the prophet went to King Hezekiah and asked, "What did those men say, and where did they come from?"

"From a distant land," Hezekiah replied. "They came to me from Babylon."

⁴The prophet asked, "What did they see in your palace?"

"They saw everything in my palace," Hezekiah said. "There is nothing among my treasures that I did not show them."

⁵Then Isaiah said to Hezekiah, "Hear the word of the LORD Almighty: ⁶The time will surely come when everything in your palace, and all that your fathers have stored up until this day, will be carried off to Babylon. Nothing will be left, says the LORD. ⁷And some of your descendants, your own flesh and blood that will be born to you, will be taken away, and they will become eunuchs in the palace of the king of Babylon."

⁸"The word of the LORD you have spoken is good," Hezekiah replied. For he thought, "There will be peace and security in my lifetime."

Comfort for God's People

40 Comfort, comfort my people,
  says your God.
²Speak tenderly to Jerusalem,
  and proclaim to her

that her hard service has been completed,
   that her sin has been paid for,
that she has received from the Lord's hand
   double for all her sins.

³A voice of one calling:
"In the desert prepare
   the way for the Lord;ᵃ
make straight in the wilderness
   a highway for our God.ᵇ
⁴Every valley shall be raised up,
   every mountain and hill made low;
the rough ground shall become level,
   the rugged places a plain.
⁵And the glory of the Lord will be revealed,
   and all mankind together will see it.
            For the mouth of the Lord has spoken."

⁶A voice says, "Cry out."
   And I said, "What shall I cry?"

"All men are like grass,
   and all their glory is like the flowers of the field.
⁷The grass withers, and the flowers fall,
   because the breath of the Lord blows on them.
   Surely the people are grass.
⁸The grass withers, and the flowers fall,
   but the word of our God stands forever."

⁹You who bring good tidings to Zion,
   go up on a high mountain.
You who bring good tidings to Jerusalem,ᶜ
   lift up your voice with a shout,

ᵃ3 Or *A voice of one calling in the desert:*
      "Prepare the way for the LORD;
ᵇ3 Hebrew; Septuagint *make straight a highway for our God.*
ᶜ9 Or *O Zion, bringer of good tidings,*
      go up on a high mountain.
   O Jerusalem, bringer of good tidings,

lift it up, do not be afraid;
say to the cities of Judah,
"Here is your God!"
¹⁰See, the Sovereign LORD comes with power,
and his arm rules for him.
See, his reward is with him,
and his recompense accompanies him.
¹¹He tends his flock like a shepherd:
He gathers the lambs in his arms
and carries them close to his heart;
he gently leads those that have young.

¹²Who has measured the waters in the hollow of
his hand,
or with the breadth of his hand marked off the
heavens?
Who has held the dust of the earth in a basket,
or weighed the mountains on the scales
and the hills in a balance?
¹³Who has understood the Spirit*a* of the LORD,
or instructed him as his counselor?
¹⁴Whom did the LORD consult to enlighten him,
and who taught him the right way?
Who was it that taught him knowledge
or showed him the path of understanding?

¹⁵Surely the nations are like a drop in the bucket;
they are regarded as dust on the scales;
he weighs the islands as though they were
fine dust.
¹⁶Lebanon is not sufficient for altar fires,
nor its animals enough for burnt offerings.
¹⁷Before him all the nations are as nothing;
they are regarded by him as worthless and less
than nothing.

a 13 Or *spirit;* or *mind*

¹⁸To whom then will you compare God?
    What image will you compare him to?
¹⁹As for an idol, a craftsman casts it,
    and a goldsmith overlays it with gold
    and fashions silver chains for it.
²⁰A man too poor to present such an offering
    selects wood that will not rot.
He looks for a skilled craftsman,
    to set up an idol that will not topple.

²¹Do you not know?
    Have you not heard?
Has it not been told you from the beginning?
    Have you not understood since the earth was
        founded?
²²He sits enthroned above the circle of the earth,
    and her people are like grasshoppers.
He stretches out the heavens like a canopy,
    and spreads them out like a tent to live in.
²³He brings princes to naught,
    and reduces the rulers of this world to nothing.
²⁴No sooner are they planted,
    no sooner are they sown,
    no sooner do they take root in the ground,
than he blows on them and they wither,
    and a whirlwind sweeps them away like
        chaff.

²⁵"To whom will you compare me?
    Or who is my equal?" says the Holy One.
²⁶Lift your eyes and look to the heavens:
    Who created all these?
He who brings out the starry host one by one,
    and calls them each by name.
Because of his great power and mighty strength,
    not one of them is missing.

²⁷Why do you say, O Jacob,
and complain, O Israel,
"My way is hidden from the LORD;
my cause is disregarded by my God"?
²⁸Do you not know?
Have you not heard?
The LORD is the everlasting God,
the Creator of the ends of the earth.
He will not grow tired or weary,
and his understanding no one can fathom.
²⁹He gives strength to the weary
and increases the power of the weak.
³⁰Even youths grow tired and weary,
and young men stumble and fall;
³¹but those who look to the LORD
will renew their strength.
They will soar on wings like eagles;
they will run and not grow weary,
they will walk and not be faint.

The Helper of Israel

41 "Be silent before me, you islands!
Let the nations renew their strength!
Let them come forward and speak;
let us meet together at the place of judgment.

²"Who has stirred up one from the east,
calling him in righteousness to his service?^a
He hands nations over to him
and subdues kings before him.
He turns them to dust with his sword,
to windblown chaff with his bow.
³He pursues them and moves on unscathed,
by a path his feet have not traveled before.
⁴Who has done this and carried it through,

---

a 2 Or *whom victory meets at every step?*

calling forth the generations from the
beginning?
I, the LORD—with the first of them
and with the last—I am he."

5The islands have seen it and fear,
the ends of the earth tremble.
They approach and come forward;
6   each helps the other
and says to his brother, "Be strong!"
7The craftsman encourages the goldsmith,
and he who smooths with the hammer
spurs on him who strikes the anvil.
He says of the welding, "It is good."
He nails down the idol so it will not topple.

8"But you, O Israel, my servant,
Jacob, whom I have chosen,
you descendants of Abraham my friend,
9I took you from the ends of the earth,
and from its farthest corners I called you.
I said, 'You are my servant';
I have chosen you and have not rejected you.
10So do not fear, for I am with you;
do not be dismayed, for I am your God.
I will strengthen you and help you;
I will uphold you with my righteous right
hand.

11"All who rage against you
will surely be ashamed and disgraced;
those who oppose you
will be as nothing and perish.
12Though you search for your enemies,
you will not find them.
Those who wage war against you
will be as nothing at all.

¹³For I am the LORD your God,
who takes hold of your right hand
and says to you, Do not fear;
I will help you.
¹⁴Do not be afraid, O worm Jacob,
O little Israel.
For I myself will help you," declares the LORD,
your Redeemer, the Holy One of Israel.
¹⁵"See, I will make you into a threshing sledge,
new and sharp, with many teeth.
You will thresh the mountains and crush them,
and reduce the hills to chaff.
¹⁶You will winnow them, the wind will pick them
up,
and a gale will blow them away.
But you will rejoice in the LORD
and glory in the Holy One of Israel.

¹⁷"The poor and needy search for water,
but there is none;
their tongues are parched with thirst.
But I the LORD will answer them;
I, the God of Israel, will not forsake them.
¹⁸I will make rivers flow on barren heights,
and springs within the valleys.
I will turn the desert into pools of water,
and the parched ground into springs.
¹⁹I will put in the desert
the cedar and the acacia, the myrtle and the
olive.
I will set pines in the wasteland,
the fir and the cypress together,
²⁰so that people may see and know,
may consider and understand,
that the hand of the LORD has done this,
that the Holy One of Israel has created it.

²¹"Present your case," says the LORD.
"Set forth your arguments," says Jacob's king.
²²"Bring in ˻your idols˼ to tell us
what is going to happen.
Tell us what the former things were,
so that we may consider them
and know their final outcome.
²³Or declare to us the things to come,
tell us what the future holds,
so we may know that you are gods.
Do something, whether good or bad,
so that we will be dismayed and filled with
fear.
²⁴But you are less than nothing
and your works are utterly worthless.
He who chooses you is detestable.

²⁵"I have stirred up one from the north, and he
comes—
one from the rising sun who calls on my
name.
He treads on rulers as if they were mortar,
as if he were a potter treading the clay.
²⁶Who told of this from the beginning, so we
could know,
or beforehand, so we could say, 'He was
right'?
No one told of this,
no one foretold it,
no one heard any words from you.
²⁷I was the first to tell Zion, 'Look, here they are!'
I gave to Jerusalem a messenger of good
tidings.
²⁸I look but there is no one—
no one among them to give counsel,
no one to give answer when I ask them.
²⁹See, they are all false!

Their deeds amount to nothing;
their images are but wind and confusion.

The Servant of the LORD

42 "Here is my servant whom I uphold,
my chosen one in whom I delight;
I will put my Spirit on him,
and he will bring justice to the nations.
²He will not shout or cry out,
or raise his voice in the streets.
³A bruised reed he will not break,
and a smoldering wick he will not snuff out.
In faithfulness he will bring forth justice;
⁴ he will not falter or be discouraged
till he establishes justice on earth.
In his law the islands will put their hope."

⁵This is what God the LORD says—
he who created the heavens and stretched them
out,
who spread out the earth and all that comes
out of it,
who gives breath to its people,
and life to those who walk on it:
⁶"I, the LORD, have called you in righteousness;
I will take hold of your hand.
I will keep you and will make you
to be a covenant for the people
and a light for the Gentiles,
⁷to open eyes that are blind,
to free captives from prison
and to release from the dungeon those who sit
in darkness.

⁸"I am the LORD; that is my name!
I will not give my glory to another
or my praise to idols.

⁹See, the former things have taken place,
  and new things I declare;
before they spring into being
  I announce them to you."

Song of Praise to the LORD

¹⁰Sing to the LORD a new song,
  his praise from the ends of the earth,
you who go down to the sea, and all that is
    in it,
    you islands, and all who live in them.
¹¹Let the desert and its towns raise their voices;
  let the settlements where Kedar lives rejoice.
Let the people of Sela sing for joy;
  let them shout from the mountaintops.
¹²Let them give glory to the LORD
  and proclaim his praise in the islands.
¹³The LORD will march out like a mighty man,
  like a warrior he will stir up his zeal;
with a shout he will raise the battle cry,
  and will triumph over his enemies.

¹⁴"For a long time I have kept silent,
  I have been quiet and held myself back.
But now, like a woman in childbirth,
  I cry out, I gasp and pant.
¹⁵I will lay waste the mountains and hills
  and dry up all their vegetation;
I will turn rivers into islands
  and dry up the pools.
¹⁶I will lead the blind by ways they have not
    known,
  along unfamiliar paths I will guide them;
I will turn the darkness into light before them
  and make the rough places smooth.
These are the things I will do;
  I will not forsake them.

¹⁷But those who trust in idols,
    who say to images, 'You are our gods,'
    will be turned back in utter shame.

Israel Blind and Deaf

¹⁸"Hear, you deaf;
    look, you blind, and see!
¹⁹Who is blind but my servant,
    and deaf like the messenger I send?
Who is blind like the one committed to me,
    blind like the servant of the LORD?
²⁰You have seen many things, but have paid no
    attention;
    your ears are open, but you hear nothing."
²¹It pleased the LORD,
    for the sake of his righteousness,
    to make his law great and glorious.
²²But this is a people plundered and looted,
    all of them trapped in pits,
    or hidden away in prisons.
They have become plunder,
    with no one to rescue them;
they have been made loot,
    with no one to say, "Send them back."

²³Which of you will listen to this,
    or pay close attention in time to come?
²⁴Who handed Jacob over to become loot,
    and Israel to the plunderers?
Was it not the LORD,
    against whom we have sinned?
For they would not follow his ways;
    they did not obey his law.
²⁵So he poured out on them his burning anger,
    the violence of war.
It enveloped them in flames, yet they did not
    understand;

it consumed them, but they did not take it to
    heart.

Israel's Only Savior

43 But now, this is what the LORD says—
    he who created you, O Jacob,
    he who formed you, O Israel:
  "Fear not, for I have redeemed you;
    I have called you by name; you are mine.
²When you pass through the waters,
    I will be with you;
and when you pass through the rivers,
    they will not sweep over you.
When you walk through the fire,
    you will not be burned;
    the flames will not set you ablaze.
³For I am the LORD, your God,
    the Holy One of Israel, your Savior;
I give Egypt for your ransom,
    Cush^a^ and Seba in your stead.
⁴Since you are precious and honored in my sight,
    and because I love you,
I will give men in exchange for you,
    and people in exchange for your life.
⁵Do not be afraid, for I am with you;
    I will bring your children from the east
    and gather you from the west.
⁶I will say to the north, 'Give them up!'
    and to the south, 'Do not hold them back.'
Bring my sons from afar,
    and my daughters from the ends of the earth—
⁷everyone who is called by my name,
    whom I created for my glory,
    whom I formed and made."

_a_ 3 That is, ancient Ethiopia

⁸Lead out those who have eyes but are blind,
who have ears but are deaf.
⁹All the nations gather together
and the peoples assemble.
Which of them foretold this
and proclaimed to us the former things?
Let them bring in their witnesses to prove they
were right,
so that others may hear and say, "It is true."
¹⁰"You are my witnesses," declares the LORD,
"and my servant whom I have chosen,
so that you may know and believe me
and understand that I am he.
Before me no god was formed,
nor will there be one after me.
¹¹I, even I, am the LORD,
and apart from me there is no savior.
¹²I have revealed and redeemed and proclaimed—
I, and not some foreign god among you.
You are my witnesses," declares the LORD, "that I
am God.
13   Yes, and from ancient days I am he.
No one can deliver out of my hand.
When I act, who can reverse it?"

God's Mercy and Israel's Unfaithfulness

¹⁴This is what the LORD says—
your Redeemer, the Holy One of Israel:
"For your sake I will send to Babylon
and bring down as fugitives all the
Chaldeans,ᵃ
in the ships in which they took pride.
¹⁵I am the LORD, your Holy One,
Israel's Creator, your king."

ᵃ *14* That is, Babylonians

¹⁶This is what the LORD says—
  he who made a way through the sea,
  a path through the mighty waters,
¹⁷who drew out the chariots and horses,
  the army and reinforcements together,
 and they lay there, never to rise again,
  extinguished, snuffed out like a wick:
¹⁸"Forget the former things;
  do not dwell on the past.
¹⁹See, I am doing a new thing!
  Now it springs up; do you not perceive it?
 I am making a way in the desert
  and streams in the wasteland.
²⁰The wild animals honor me,
  the jackals and the ostriches,
 because I provide water in the desert
  and streams in the wasteland,
 to give drink to my people, my chosen,
²¹ the people I formed for myself
  that they may recount my praise.

²²"Yet you have not called upon me, O Jacob,
  you have not wearied yourselves for me,
   O Israel.
²³You have not brought me sheep for burnt
    offerings,
  nor honored me with your sacrifices.
 I have not burdened you with grain offerings,
  nor wearied you with demands for incense.
²⁴You have not bought any fragrant calamus for
    me,
  or lavished on me the fat of your sacrifices.
 But you have burdened me with your sins
  and wearied me with your offenses.

²⁵"I, even I, am he who blots out
  your transgressions, for my own sake,

and remembers your sins no more.
²⁶Review the past for me,
    let us argue the matter together;
    state the case for your innocence.
²⁷Your first father sinned;
    your spokesmen rebelled against me.
²⁸So I will disgrace the dignitaries of your temple,
    and I will consign Jacob to destruction^a
    and Israel to scorn.

Israel the Chosen

44 "But now listen, O Jacob, my servant,
    Israel, whom I have chosen.
²This is what the LORD says—
    he who made you, who formed you in the
        womb,
    and who will help you:
 Do not be afraid, O Jacob, my servant,
    Jeshurun, whom I have chosen.
³For I will pour water on the thirsty land,
    and streams on the dry ground;
 I will pour out my Spirit on your offspring,
    and my blessing on your descendants.
⁴They will spring up like grass in a meadow,
    like poplar trees by flowing streams.
⁵One will say, 'I belong to the LORD';
    another will call himself by the name of Jacob;
 still another will write on his hand, 'The LORD's,'
    and will take the name Israel.

The LORD, Not Idols

⁶"This is what the LORD says—
    Israel's king and Redeemer, the LORD Almighty:
    I am the first and I am the last;

---

^a 28 The Hebrew term refers to the practice of devoting things or persons irrevocably to the LORD, often by total destruction.

apart from me there is no God.
7Who then is like me? Let him proclaim it.
   Let him declare and lay out before me
what has happened since I established my
         ancient people,
      and what is yet to come—
      yes, let him foretell what will come.
8Do not tremble, do not be afraid.
   Did I not proclaim this and foretell it long ago?
   You are my witnesses. Is there any God besides
         me?
      No, there is no other Rock; I know not one."

9All who make idols are nothing,
   and the things they treasure are worthless.
   Those who would speak up for them are blind;
      they are ignorant, to their own shame.
10Who shapes a god and casts an idol,
   which can profit him nothing?
11He and his kind will be put to shame;
   craftsmen are nothing but men.
   Let them all come together and take their stand;
      they will be brought down to terror and
         infamy.

12The blacksmith takes a tool
   and works with it in the coals;
   he shapes an idol with hammers,
      he forges it with the might of his arm.
   He gets hungry and loses his strength;
      he drinks no water and grows faint.
13The carpenter measures with a line
   and makes an outline with a marker;
   he roughs it out with chisels
      and marks it with compasses.
   He shapes it in the form of man,
      of man in all his glory,

that it may dwell in a shrine.
¹⁴He cut down cedars,
 or perhaps took a cypress or oak.
He let it grow among the trees of the forest,
 or planted a pine, and the rain made it grow.
¹⁵It is man's fuel for burning;
 some of it he takes and warms himself,
 he kindles a fire and bakes bread.
But he also fashions a god and worships it;
 he makes an idol and bows down to it.
¹⁶Half of it he burns in the fire;
 over it he prepares his meal,
 he roasts his meat and eats his fill.
He also warms himself and says, "Ah!
 I am warm; I have felt the fire."
¹⁷From the rest he makes a god, his idol;
 he bows down to it and worships.
He prays to it and says,
 "Save me; you are my god."
¹⁸They know nothing, they understand nothing;
 their eyes are plastered over so they cannot
  see,
 and their minds closed so they cannot
  understand.
¹⁹No one stops to think,
 no one has the knowledge or understanding to
  say,
"Half of it I used for fuel;
 I even baked bread over its coals,
 I roasted meat and I ate.
Shall I make a detestable thing from what is
  left?
 Shall I bow down to a block of wood?"
²⁰He feeds on ashes, a deluded heart misleads
  him;
 he cannot save himself, or say,
 "Is not this thing in my right hand a lie?"

²¹"Remember these things, O Jacob,
    for you are my servant, O Israel.
I have made you, you are my servant;
    O Israel, I will not forget you.
²²I have swept away your offenses like a cloud,
    your sins like the morning mist.
Return to me,
    for I have redeemed you."

²³Sing for joy, O heavens, for the LORD has done
        this;
    shout aloud, O earth beneath.
Burst out into song, you mountains,
    you forests and all your trees.
For the LORD has redeemed Jacob,
    he displays his glory in Israel.

Jerusalem to Be Inhabited

²⁴"This is what the LORD says—
    your Redeemer, who formed you in the womb:

I am the LORD,
who has made all things,
who alone stretched out the heavens,
who spread out the earth by myself,

²⁵who foils the signs of false prophets
    and makes fools of diviners,
who overthrows the learning of the wise
    and turns it into nonsense;
²⁶who carries out the words of his servants,
    and fulfills the predictions of his messengers,

who says of Jerusalem, 'It shall be inhabited,'
    of the cities of Judah, 'They shall be built,'
    and of their ruins, 'I will restore them,'
²⁷who says to the watery deep, 'Be dry,
    and I will dry up your streams,'

²⁸who says of Cyrus, 'He is my shepherd
    and will accomplish all that I please;
    he will say of Jerusalem, "Let it be rebuilt,"
    and of the temple, "Let its foundations be
        laid." '

45 "This is what the LORD says to his anointed,
    to Cyrus, whose right hand I take hold of
to subdue nations before him
    and to strip kings of their armor,
to open doors before him
    so that gates will not be shut:
²I will go before you
    and will level the mountains;ᵃ
I will break down gates of bronze
    and cut through bars of iron.
³I will give you the treasures of darkness,
    riches stored in secret places,
so that you may know that I am the LORD,
    the God of Israel, who calls you by name.
⁴For the sake of Jacob my servant,
    of Israel my chosen,
I call you by name
    and bestow on you a title of honor,
    though you do not acknowledge me.
⁵I am the LORD, and there is no other;
    apart from me there is no God.
I will strengthen you,
    though you have not acknowledged me,
⁶so that from the rising of the sun
    to the place of its setting
men may know there is none besides me.
    I am the LORD, and there is no other.
⁷I form the light and create darkness,

ᵃ 2 Dead Sea Scrolls and Septuagint; the meaning of the word in the Masoretic Text
is uncertain.

I bring prosperity and create disaster;
  I, the LORD, do all these things.

8"You heavens above, rain down righteousness;
  let the clouds shower it down.
Let the earth open wide,
  let salvation spring up,
let righteousness grow with it;
  I, the LORD, have created it.

9"Woe to him who quarrels with his Maker,
  to him who is but a potsherd among the
    potsherds on the ground.
Does the clay say to the potter,
  'What are you making?'
Does your work say,
  'He has no hands'?
10Woe to him who says to his father,
  'What have you begotten?'
or to his mother,
  'What have you brought to birth?'

11"This is what the LORD says—
  the Holy One of Israel, and its Maker:
Concerning things to come,
  do you question me about my children,
  or give me orders about the work of my
    hands?
12It is I who made the earth
  and created mankind upon it.
My own hands stretched out the heavens;
  I marshaled their starry hosts.
13I will raise up Cyrus^a in my righteousness:
  I will make all his ways straight.
He will rebuild my city

^a 13 Hebrew *him*

and set my exiles free,
but not for a price or reward,
     says the LORD Almighty."

¹⁴This is what the LORD says:

"The products of Egypt and the merchandise of
     Cush,ᵃ
and those tall Sabeans—
they will come over to you
     and will be yours;
they will trudge behind you,
     coming over to you in chains.
They will bow down before you
     and plead with you, saying,
'Surely God is with you, and there is no other;
     there is no other god.'"

¹⁵Truly you are a God who hides himself,
     O God and Savior of Israel.
¹⁶All the makers of idols will be put to shame and
     disgraced;
they will go off into disgrace together.
¹⁷But Israel will be saved by the LORD
     with an everlasting salvation;
you will never be put to shame or disgraced,
     to ages everlasting.

¹⁸For this is what the LORD says—
he who created the heavens,
     he is God;
he who fashioned and made the earth,
     he founded it;
he did not create it to be empty,
     but formed it to be inhabited—
he says:

ᵃ 14 That is, ancient Ethiopia

"I am the LORD,
and there is no other.
¹⁹I have not spoken in secret,
from somewhere in a land of darkness;
I have not said to Jacob's descendants,
'Seek me in vain.'
I, the LORD, speak the truth;
I declare what is right.

²⁰"Gather together and come;
assemble, you fugitives from the nations.
Ignorant are those who carry about idols of
wood,
who pray to gods that cannot save.
²¹Declare what is to be, present it—
let them take counsel together.
Who foretold this long ago,
who declared it from the distant past?
Was it not I, the LORD?
And there is no God apart from me,
a righteous God and a Savior;
there is none but me.

²²"Turn to me and be saved,
all you ends of the earth;
for I am God, and there is no other.
²³By myself I have sworn on oath,
my mouth has uttered in all integrity
a word that will not be revoked:
Before me every knee will bow;
by me every tongue will swear.
²⁴They will say of me, 'In the LORD alone
are righteousness and strength.' "
All who have raged against him
will come to him and be put to shame.
²⁵But in the LORD all the descendants of Israel
will be found righteous and will exult.

Gods of Babylon

46

Bel bows down, Nebo stoops low;
   their idols are borne by beasts of burden.[a]
The images that are carried about are
      burdensome,
   a burden for the weary.
²They stoop and bow down together;
   unable to rescue the burden,
   they themselves go off into captivity.

³"Listen to me, house of Jacob,
   all you who remain of the house of Israel,
you whom I have upheld since you were
      conceived,
   and have carried since your birth.
⁴Even to your old age and gray hairs
   I am he, I am he who will sustain you.
I have made you and I will carry you;
   I will sustain you and I will rescue you.

⁵"To whom will you compare me or count me
      equal?
   To whom will you liken me that we may be
      compared?
⁶Some pour out gold from their bags
   and weigh out silver on the scales;
they hire a goldsmith to make it into a god,
   and they bow down and worship it.
⁷They lift it and carry it on their shoulders;
   they set it up in its place, and there it
      stands.
   From that spot it cannot move.
Though one cries out to it, it does not answer;
   it cannot save him from his troubles.

a 1 Or *are but beasts and cattle.*

8"Remember this, fix it in mind,
    take it to heart, you rebels.
9Remember the former things, those of long ago;
    I am God, and there is no other;
    I am God, and there is none like me.
10I make known the end from the beginning,
    from ancient times what is still to come.
I say: My purpose will stand,
    and I will do all that I please.
11From the east I summon a bird of prey;
    from a far-off land, a man to fulfill my
        purpose.
What I have said, that will I bring about;
    what I have planned, that will I do.
12Listen to me, you stubborn-hearted,
    you who are far from righteousness.
13I am bringing my righteousness near;
    it is not far away;
    and my salvation will not be delayed.
I will grant salvation to Zion,
    my splendor to Israel.

The Fall of Babylon

47 "Go down, sit in the dust,
    Virgin Daughter of Babylon;
sit on the ground without a throne,
    Daughter of the Chaldeans.a
No more will you be called
    tender or delicate.
2Take millstones and grind flour;
    take off your veil.
Lift up your skirts, bare your legs,
    and wade through the streams.
3Your nakedness will be exposed
    and your shame uncovered.

a 1 That is, Babylonians

113

I will take vengeance;
  I will spare no one."

⁴Our Redeemer—the LORD Almighty is his
    name—
  is the Holy One of Israel.

⁵"Sit in silence, go into darkness,
    Daughter of the Chaldeansᵃ;
  no more will you be called
    queen of kingdoms.
⁶I was angry with my people
    and desecrated my heritage;
  I gave them into your hand,
    and you showed them no mercy.
  Even on the aged
    you laid a very heavy yoke.
⁷You said, 'I will continue forever—
    the eternal queen!'
  But you did not consider these things
    or reflect on what might happen.

⁸"Now then, listen, you wanton creature,
    lounging in your security
  and saying to yourself,
    'I am, and there is none besides me.
  I will never be a widow
    or suffer the loss of children.'
⁹Both of these will overtake you,
    in a moment, on a single day:
    loss of children and widowhood.
  They will come upon you in full measure,
    in spite of your many sorceries
    and all your potent spells.

ᵃ 5 That is, Babylonians

[10]You have trusted in your wickedness
    and have said, 'No one sees me.'
Your wisdom and knowledge mislead you,
    when you say to yourself,
    'I am, and there is none besides me.'
[11]Disaster will come upon you,
    and you will not know how to conjure it
        away.
A calamity will fall upon you
    that you cannot ward off with a ransom;
a catastrophe you cannot foresee
    will suddenly come upon you.

[12]"Keep on, then, with your magic spells
    and with your many sorceries,
    which you have labored at since childhood.
Perhaps you will succeed,
    perhaps you will cause terror.
[13]All the counsel you have received has only worn
        you out!
Let your astrologers come forward,
those stargazers who make predictions month by
        month,
    let them save you from what is coming upon
        you.
[14]Surely they are like stubble;
    the fire will burn them up.
They cannot even save themselves
    from the power of the flame.
Here are no coals to warm anyone;
    here is no fire to sit by.
[15]That is all they can do for you—
    these you have labored with
    and trafficked with since childhood.
Everyone of them goes on in his error;
    there is not one that can save you.

Stubborn Israel

48 "Listen to this, O house of Jacob,
      you who are called by the name of Israel
      and come from the line of Judah,
   you who take oaths in the name of the LORD
      and invoke the God of Israel—
      but not in truth or righteousness—
²you who call yourselves citizens of the holy city
      and rely on the God of Israel—
      the LORD Almighty is his name:
³I foretold the former things long ago,
      my mouth announced them and I made them
         known;
      then suddenly I acted, and they came to pass.
⁴For I knew how stubborn you were;
      the sinews of your neck were iron,
      your forehead was bronze.
⁵Therefore I told you these things long ago;
      before they happened I announced them to
         you
   so that you could not say,
      'My idols did them;
      my wooden image and metal god ordained
         them.'
⁶You have heard these things; prophesy them all.
      Will you not declare them?

   "From now on I will tell you of new things,
      of hidden things unknown to you.
⁷They are created now, and not long ago;
      you have not heard of them before today.
   So you cannot say,
      'Yes, I knew of them.'
⁸You have neither heard nor understood;
      from of old your ear has not been open.
   Well do I know how treacherous you are;

you were called a rebel from birth.
⁹For my own name's sake I delay my wrath;
    for the sake of my praise I hold it back from
      you,
    so as not to cut you off.
¹⁰See, I have refined you, though not as silver;
    I have tested you in the furnace of affliction.
¹¹For my own sake, for my own sake, I do this.
    How can I let myself be defamed?
    I will not yield my glory to another.

Israel Freed

¹²"Listen to me, O Jacob,
    Israel, whom I have called:
I am he;
    I am the first and I am the last.
¹³My own hand laid the foundations of the earth,
    and my right hand spread out the heavens;
when I summon them,
    they all stand up together.

¹⁴"Assemble, all of you, and listen:
    Which of ˌthe idolsˌ has foretold these things?
The LORD's chosen ally
    will carry out his purpose against Babylon;
    his arm will be against the Chaldeans.ᵃ
¹⁵I, even I, have spoken;
    yes, I have called him.
I will bring him,
    and he will succeed in his mission.

¹⁶"Come near me and listen to this:

From the first announcement I have not spoken
    in secret;
    at the time it happens I am there."

ᵃ *14* That is, Babylonians

And now the Sovereign Lord has sent me,
   with his Spirit.

¹⁷This is what the Lord says—
   your Redeemer, the Holy One of Israel:
"I am the Lord your God,
   who teaches you what is beneficial,
   who directs you in the way you should go.
¹⁸If only you had paid attention to my commands,
   your peace would have been like a river,
   your righteousness like the waves of the sea.
¹⁹Your descendants would have been like the
     sand,
   your children like its numberless grains;
their name would never be cut off,
   nor destroyed from before me."

²⁰Leave Babylon,
   flee from the Chaldeans[a]!
Announce this with shouts of joy
   and proclaim it.
Send it out to the ends of the earth;
   say, "The Lord has redeemed his servant
     Jacob."
²¹They did not thirst when he led them through
     the deserts;
   he made water flow for them from the
     rock;
he split the rock
   and water gushed out.

²²"There is no peace," says the Lord, "for the
   wicked."

---

a 20 That is, Babylonians

The Servant of the LORD

49 Listen to me, you islands;
　　hear this you distant nations:
　Before I was born the LORD called me;
　　from my birth he has made mention of my
　　　name.
²He made my mouth like a sharpened sword,
　　in the shadow of his hand he hid me;
　he made me into a polished arrow
　　and concealed me in his quiver.
³He said to me, "You are my servant—
　　Israel, in whom I will display my splendor."
⁴But I said, "I have labored to no purpose;
　　I have spent my strength in vain and for
　　　nothing.
　Yet what is due me is in the LORD's hand,
　　and my reward is with my God."

⁵And now the LORD says—
　　he who formed me in the womb to be his
　　　servant
　to bring Jacob back to him
　　and gather Israel again to himself,
　for I am honored in the eyes of the LORD
　　and my God has been my strength—
⁶he says:
　"It is too small a thing for you to be my servant
　　to restore the tribes of Jacob
　　and bring back those of Israel I have kept.
　I will also make you a light for the Gentiles,
　　that you may bring my salvation to the ends
　　　of the earth."

⁷This is what the LORD says—
　　the Redeemer and Holy One of Israel—
　to him who was despised and abhorred by the
　　　nation,

to the servant of rulers:
"Kings will see you and arise,
  princes will see and bow down,
because of the LORD, who is faithful,
  the Holy One of Israel, who has chosen you."

Restoration of Israel

⁸This is what the LORD says:

"In the time of my favor I will answer you,
  and in the day of salvation I will help you;
I will keep you and will make you
  to be a covenant for the people,
  to restore the land
and to reassign its desolate inheritances,
⁹to say to the captives, 'Come out,'
  and to those in darkness, 'Be free!'

"They will feed beside the roads
  and find pasture on every barren hill.
¹⁰They will neither hunger nor thirst,
  nor will the desert heat or the sun beat upon
    them.
He who has compassion on them will guide
    them
  and lead them beside springs of water.
¹¹I will turn all my mountains into roads,
  and my highways will be raised up.
¹²See, they will come from afar—
  some from the north, some from the west,
  some from the region of Sinim.^a"

¹³Shout for joy, O heavens;
  rejoice, O earth;
  burst into song, O mountains!

---

^a 12 Or *Syene*; that is, Aswan (see Dead Sea Scrolls)

For the LORD comforts his people
and will have compassion on his afflicted ones.

¹⁴But Zion said, "The LORD has forsaken me,
the Lord has forgotten me."

¹⁵"Can a mother forget the baby at her breast
and have no compassion on the child she has
borne?
Though she may forget,
I will not forget you!
¹⁶See, I have engraved you on the palms of my
hands;
your walls are ever before me.
¹⁷Your sons hasten back,
and those who laid you waste depart from
you.
¹⁸Lift up your eyes and look around;
all your sons gather and come to you.
As I live," declares the LORD,
"you will wear them all as ornaments;
you will put them on, like a bride.

¹⁹"Though you were ruined and made desolate
and your land laid waste,
now you will be too small for your people,
and those who devoured you will be far away.
²⁰The children born during your bereavement
will yet say in your hearing,
'This place is too small for us;
give us more space to live in.'
²¹Then you will say in your heart,
'Who bore me these?
I was bereaved and barren;
I was exiled and rejected.
Who brought these up?
I was left all alone,

but these—where have they come from?' "

²²This is what the Sovereign LORD says:

"See, I will beckon to the Gentiles,
  I will lift up my banner to the peoples;
they will bring your sons in their arms
  and carry your daughters on their shoulders.
²³Kings will be your foster fathers,
  and their queens your nursing mothers.
They will bow down before you with their faces
    to the ground;
  they will lick the dust at your feet.
Then you will know that I am the LORD;
  those who look to me will not be
    disappointed."

²⁴Can plunder be taken from warriors,
  or captives rescued from the fierce^a?

²⁵But this is what the LORD says:

"Yes, captives will be taken from warriors,
  and plunder retrieved from the fierce;
I will contend with those who contend with you,
  and your children I will save.
²⁶I will make your oppressors eat their own flesh;
  they will be drunk on their own blood, as
    with wine.
Then all mankind will know
  that I, the LORD, am your Savior,
  your Redeemer, the Mighty One of Jacob."

Israel's Sin and the Servant's Obedience

50 This is what the LORD says:
  "Where is your mother's certificate of divorce
    with which I sent her away?

^a 24 Dead Sea Scrolls and some ancient versions; Masoretic Text *righteous*

Or to which of my creditors
  did I sell you?
Because of your sins you were sold;
    because of your transgressions your mother
      was sent away.
²When I came, why was there no one?
    When I called, why was there no one to
      answer?
Was my arm too short to ransom you?
    Do I lack the strength to rescue you?
By a mere rebuke I dry up the sea,
  I turn rivers into a desert;
their fish rot for lack of water
  and die of thirst.
³I clothe the sky with darkness
  and make sackcloth its covering."

⁴The Sovereign LORD has given me an instructed
      tongue,
    to know the word that sustains the weary.
 He wakens me morning by morning,
    wakens my ear to listen like one being taught.
⁵The Sovereign LORD has opened my ears,
    and I have not been rebellious;
    I have not drawn back.
⁶I offered my back to those who beat me,
    my cheeks to those who pulled out my beard;
 I did not hide my face
    from mocking and spitting.
⁷Because the Sovereign LORD helps me,
    I will not be disgraced.
 Therefore have I set my face like flint,
    and I know I will not be put to shame.
⁸He who vindicates me is near.
    Who then will bring charges against me?
    Let us face each other!
Who is my accuser?

Let him confront me!
⁹It is the Sovereign LORD who helps me.
  Who is he that will condemn me?
They will all wear out like a garment;
  the moths will eat them up.

¹⁰Who among you fears the LORD
  and obeys the word of his servant?
Let him who walks in the dark,
  who has no light,
trust in the name of the LORD
  and rely on his God.
¹¹But now, all you who light fires
  and provide yourselves with flaming torches,
go, walk in the light of your fires
  and of the torches you have set ablaze.
This is what you shall receive from my hand:
  You will lie down in torment.

Everlasting Salvation for Zion

51 "Listen to me, you who pursue righteousness
  and who seek the LORD:
Look to the rock from which you were cut,
  and to the quarry from which you were
    hewn;
²look to Abraham, your father,
  and to Sarah, who gave you birth.
When I called him he was but one,
  and I blessed him and made him many.
³The LORD will surely comfort Zion
  and will look with compassion on all her
    ruins;
he will make her deserts like Eden,
  her wastelands like the garden of the LORD.
Joy and gladness will be found in her,
  thanksgiving and the sound of singing.

⁴"Hear me, my people;
  give ear to me, my nation:
The law will go out from me;
  my justice will become a light to the nations.
⁵My righteousness draws near speedily,
  my salvation is on the way,
  and my arm will bring justice to the nations.
The islands will look to me
  and wait in hope for my arm.
⁶Lift up your eyes to the heavens,
  look at the earth beneath;
the heavens will vanish like smoke,
  the earth will wear out like a garment
  and its inhabitants die like flies.
But my salvation will last forever,
  my righteousness will never fail.

⁷"Hear me, you who know what is right,
  you people who have my law in your hearts:
Do not fear the reproach of men
  or be terrified by their insults.
⁸For the moth will eat them up like a garment;
  the worm will devour them like wool.
But my righteousness will last forever,
  my salvation through all generations."

⁹Awake, awake! Clothe yourself with strength,
  O arm of the Lord;
awake, as in days gone by,
  as in generations of old.
Was it not you who cut Rahab to pieces,
  who pierced that monster through?
¹⁰Was it not you who dried up the sea,
  the waters of the great deep,
who made a road in the depths of the sea
  so that the redeemed might cross over?
¹¹The ransomed of the Lord will return.

They will enter Zion with singing;
    everlasting joy will crown their heads.
Gladness and joy will overtake them,
    and sorrow and sighing will flee away.

¹²"I, even I, am he who comforts you.
    Who are you that you fear mortal men,
    the sons of men, who are but grass,
¹³that you forget the LORD your Maker,
    who stretched out the heavens
    and laid the foundations of the earth,
that you live in constant terror every day
    because of the wrath of the oppressor,
    who is bent on destruction?
For where is the wrath of the oppressor?
¹⁴ The cowering prisoners will soon be set free;
    they will not die in their dungeon,
    nor will they lack bread.
¹⁵For I am the LORD your God,
    who churns up the sea so that its waves
      roar—
    the LORD Almighty is his name.
¹⁶I have put my words in your mouth
    and covered you with the shadow of my
      hand—
I who set the heavens in place,
    who laid the foundations of the earth,
    and who say to Zion, 'You are my people.' "

The Cup of the LORD's Wrath

¹⁷Awake, awake!
    Rise up, O Jerusalem,
you who have drunk from the hand of the LORD
    the cup of his wrath,
you who have drained to its dregs
    the goblet that makes men stagger.
¹⁸Of all the sons she bore

there was none to guide her;
of all the sons she reared
there was none to take her by the hand.
¹⁹These double calamities have come upon you—
who can comfort you?—
ruin and destruction, famine and sword—
who can*a* console you?
²⁰Your sons have fainted;
they lie at the head of every street,
like an antelope caught in a net.
They are filled with the wrath of the LORD
and the rebuke of your God.

²¹Therefore hear this, you afflicted one,
made drunk, but not with wine.
²²This is what your Sovereign LORD says,
your God, who defends his people:
"See, I have taken out of your hand
the cup that made you stagger;
from that cup, the goblet of my wrath,
you will never drink again.
²³I will put it into the hands of your tormentors,
who said to you,
'Fall prostrate that we may walk over you.'
And you made your back like the ground,
like a street to be walked over."

52 Awake, awake, O Zion,
clothe yourself with strength.
Put on your garments of splendor,
O Jerusalem, the holy city.
The uncircumcised and defiled
will not enter you again.
²Shake off your dust;
rise up, sit enthroned, O Jerusalem.

a 19 Dead Sea Scrolls and ancient versions; Masoretic Text *how can I*

Free yourself from the chains on your neck,
   O captive Daughter of Zion.

³For this is what the LORD says:

"You were sold for nothing,
   and without money you will be redeemed."

⁴For this is what the Sovereign LORD says:

"At first my people went down to Egypt to live;
   lately, Assyria has oppressed them."

⁵"And now whom do I have here?" declares the LORD.

"For my people have been taken away for
     nothing,
   and those who rule them mock,ᵃ"
                 declares the LORD.
"And all the day long
   my name is constantly blasphemed.
⁶Therefore my people will know my name;
   therefore in that day they will know
that it is I who foretold it.
   Yes, it is I."

⁷How beautiful on the mountains
   are the feet of those who bring good news,
who proclaim peace,
   who bring good tidings,
   who proclaim salvation,
who say to Zion,
   "Your God reigns!"
⁸Listen! Your watchmen lift up their voices;
   together they shout for joy.
When the LORD returns to Zion,
   they will see it with their own eyes.
⁹Burst into songs of joy together,

ᵃ 5 Dead Sea Scrolls and some ancient versions; Masoretic Text *wail*

you ruins of Jerusalem,
for the LORD has comforted his people,
he has redeemed Jerusalem.
¹⁰The LORD will lay bare his holy arm
in the sight of all the nations,
and all the ends of the earth will see
the salvation of our God.

¹¹Depart, depart, go out from there!
Touch no unclean thing!
Come out from it and be pure,
you who carry the vessels of the LORD.
¹²But you will not leave in haste,
or go in flight;
for the LORD will go before you,
the God of Israel will be your rear guard.

The Suffering and Glory of the Servant

¹³See, my servant will act wisely;[a]
he will be raised and lifted up and highly
exalted.
¹⁴Just as there were many who were appalled at
him[b]—
his appearance was so disfigured beyond that
of any man
and his form marred beyond human likeness—
¹⁵so will he sprinkle many nations,[c]
and kings will shut their mouths because of
him.
For those who were not told will see,
and those who have not heard will
understand.

---

[a] 13 Or *will prosper;*　　[b] 14 Hebrew *you*　　[c] 15 Hebrew; Septuagint *so will many nations marvel at him,*

53 Who has believed our message
   and to whom has the arm of the LORD been
      revealed?
²He grew up before him like a tender shoot,
   and like a root out of dry ground.
He had no beauty or majesty to attract us to him,
   nothing in his appearance that we should
      desire him.
³He was despised and rejected by men,
   a man of sorrows, and familiar with suffering.
Like one from whom men hide their faces
   he was despised, and we esteemed him not.

⁴Surely he took up our infirmities
   and carried our sorrows,
yet we considered him stricken by God,
   smitten by him, and afflicted.
⁵But he was pierced for our transgressions,
   he was crushed for our iniquities;
the punishment that brought us peace was upon
      him,
   and by his wounds we are healed.
⁶All we, like sheep, have gone astray,
   each of us has turned to his own way;
and the LORD has laid on him
   the iniquity of us all.

⁷He was oppressed and afflicted,
   yet he did not open his mouth;
he was led like a lamb to the slaughter,
   and as a sheep before her shearers is silent,
   so he did not open his mouth.
⁸By oppressionᵃ and judgment, he was taken
      away.

ᵃ 8 Or *From arrest*

And who can speak of his descendants?
For he was cut off from the land of the living;
    for the transgression of my people he was
        stricken.[a]
⁹He was assigned a grave with the wicked,
    and with the rich in his death,
though he had done no violence,
    nor was any deceit in his mouth.

¹⁰Although it was the LORD's will to crush him
    and cause him to suffer,
    and though the LORD makes[b] his life a guilt
        offering,
he will see his offspring and prolong his days,
    and the will of the LORD will prosper in his
        hand.
¹¹After the suffering of his soul,
    he will see the light of life[c] and be satisfied;[d]
by his knowledge[e] my righteous servant will
        justify many,
    and he will bear their iniquities.
¹²Therefore I will give him a portion among the
        great,
    and he will divide the spoils with the strong,
because he poured out his life unto death,
    and was numbered with the transgressors.
For he bore the sin of many,
    and made intercession for the transgressors.

---

[a] 8 Or   *Yet who of his generation considered*
    that he was cut off from the land of the living
    for the transgression of my people,
    to whom the blow was due?
[b] 10 Hebrew *though you make*   [c] 11 Dead Sea Scrolls and Septuagint; Masoretic
Text omits *the light of life.*   [d] 11 Or (with Masoretic Text) *he will see the result of
the suffering of his soul and be satisfied;*   [e] 11 Or *by knowledge of him*

The Future Glory of Zion

54 "Sing, O barren woman,
    you who never bore a child;
burst into song, shout for joy,
    you who were never in labor;
because more are the children of the desolate
        woman
    than of her who has a husband,"

                                    says the LORD.

²"Enlarge the place of your tent,
    stretch your tent curtains wide,
    do not hold back;
lengthen your cords,
    strengthen your stakes.
³For you will spread out to the right and to the
        left;
    your descendants will dispossess nations
    and settle in their desolate cities.

⁴"Do not be afraid; you will not suffer shame.
    Do not fear disgrace; you will not be
        humiliated.
You will forget the shame of your youth
    and remember no more the reproach of your
        widowhood.
⁵For your Maker is your husband—
    the LORD Almighty is his name—
the Holy One of Israel is your Redeemer;
    he is called the God of all the earth.
⁶The LORD will call you back
    as if you were a wife deserted and distressed
        in spirit—
a wife who married young,
    only to be rejected," says your God.
⁷"For a brief moment I abandoned you,

but with deep compassion I will bring you
    back.
⁸In a surge of anger
    I hid my face from you for a moment,
but with everlasting kindness
    I will have compassion on you,"
    says the LORD your Redeemer.

⁹"To me this is like the days of Noah,
    when I swore that the waters of Noah would
        never again cover the earth.
So now I have sworn not to be angry with you,
    nor ever to rebuke you again.
¹⁰Though the mountains be shaken
    and the hills be removed,
yet my unfailing love for you will not be shaken,
    nor my covenant of peace be removed,"
    says the LORD, who has compassion on you.

¹¹"O afflicted city, lashed by storms and not
        comforted,
    I will build you with stones of turquoise,
    your foundations with sapphires.
¹²I will make your battlements of rubies,
    your gates of sparkling jewels,
    and all your walls of precious stones.
¹³All your sons will be taught by the LORD,
    and great will be your children's peace.
¹⁴In righteousness you will be established:
    Tyranny will be far from you;
        you will have nothing to fear.
    Terror will be far removed;
        it will not come near you.
¹⁵If anyone does attack you, it will not be my
        doing;
    whoever attacks you will fall because of you.

16"See, it is I who created the blacksmith
who fans the coals into flame
and forges a weapon fit for its work.
And it is I who have created the destroyer to
work havoc;
17 no weapon forged against you will prevail,
and you will refute every tongue that accuses
you.
This is the heritage of the servants of the LORD,
and this is their vindication from me," declares
the LORD.

Invitation to the Thirsty

55 "Come, all you who are thirsty,
come to the waters;
and you who have no money,
come, buy and eat!
Come, buy wine and milk
without money and without cost.
2Why spend money on what is not bread,
and your labor on what does not satisfy?
Listen, listen to me, and eat what is good,
and your soul will delight in the richest of
fare.
3Give ear and come to me;
hear me, that your soul may live.
I will make an everlasting covenant with you,
my unfailing kindnesses promised to David.
4See, I have made him a witness to the peoples,
a leader and commander of the peoples.
5Surely you will summon nations you know not,
and nations that do not know you will hasten
to you,
because of the LORD your God,
the Holy One of Israel,
for he has endowed you with splendor."

⁶Seek the LORD while he may be found;
  call on him while he is near.
⁷Let the wicked forsake his way
  and the evil man his thoughts.
 Let him turn to the LORD, and he will have
    mercy on him,
  and to our God, for he will freely pardon.

⁸"For my thoughts are not your thoughts,
  neither are your ways my ways,"
                    declares the LORD.
⁹"As the heavens are higher than the earth,
  so are my ways higher than your ways
  and my thoughts than your thoughts.
¹⁰As the rain and the snow
  come down from heaven,
 and do not return to it,
  without watering the earth
 and making it bud and flourish,
  so that it yields seed for sowing and bread for
    eating,
¹¹so is my word that goes out from my mouth:
  It will not return to me empty,
 but shall accomplish what I desire
  and achieve the purpose for which I sent it.
¹²You will go out in joy
  and be led forth in peace;
 the mountains and hills
  will burst into song before you,
 and all the trees of the field
  will clap their hands.
¹³Instead of the thornbush will grow the pine tree;
  and instead of briers the myrtle will grow.
 This will be for the LORD's renown,
  for an everlasting sign
  which will not be destroyed."

Salvation for Others

56 This is what the LORD says:

"Maintain justice
  and do what is right,
 for my salvation is close at hand
  and my righteousness will soon be revealed.
²Blessed is the man who does this,
  the man who holds it fast,
 who keeps the Sabbath without profaning it,
  and keeps his hand from doing any evil."

³Let no foreigner who has joined himself to the
   LORD say,
  "The LORD will surely exclude me from his
   people."
 And let not any eunuch complain,
  "I am only a dry tree."

⁴For this is what the LORD says:

 "To the eunuchs who keep my Sabbaths,
  who choose what pleases me
  and hold fast to my covenant—
⁵to them I will give within my temple and its
   walls
  a memorial and a name
  better than sons and daughters;
 I will give them an everlasting name
  that will not be cut off.
⁶And foreigners who bind themselves to the LORD
   to serve him,
  to love the name of the LORD,
  and to worship him,
 who keep the Sabbath without profaning it
  and who hold fast to my covenant—
⁷these I will bring to my holy mountain
  and give them joy in my house of prayer.

Their burnt offerings and sacrifices
    will be accepted on my altar;
for my house will be called
    a house of prayer for all nations."
8The Sovereign LORD declares—
    he who gathers the exiles of Israel:
"I will gather still others to them
    besides those already gathered."

God's Accusation Against the Wicked

9Come, all you beasts of the field,
    come and devour, all you beasts of the
        forest!
10Israel's watchmen are blind,
    they all lack knowledge;
they are all mute dogs,
    they cannot bark;
dreaming and lying around,
    they love to sleep.
11They are dogs with mighty appetites;
    they never have enough.
They are shepherds who lack understanding;
    they all turn to their own way,
    each seeks his own gain.
12"Come," each one cries, "let me get wine;
    let us drink our fill!
And tomorrow will be like today,
    or even far better."

57 The righteous perish,
    and no one ponders it in his heart;
devout men are taken away,
    and no one understands
that the righteous are taken away
    to be spared from evil.
2Those who walk uprightly
    enter into peace;

they find rest as they lie in death.

³"But you—come here, you sons of a sorceress,
you offspring of adulterers and prostitutes!
⁴Whom are you mocking?
At whom do you sneer
and stick out your tongue?
Are you not a brood of rebels,
the offspring of liars?
⁵You burn with lust among the oaks
and under every spreading tree;
you sacrifice your children in the ravines
and under the overhanging crags.
⁶⌞The idols⌟ among the smooth stones of the
ravines are your portion;
they, they are your lot.
Yes, to them you have poured out drink
offerings
and offered grain offerings.
In light of these things, should I relent?
⁷You have made your bed on a high and lofty
hill;
there you went up to offer your sacrifices.
⁸Behind your doors and your doorposts
you have put your pagan symbols.
Forsaking me, you uncovered your bed,
you climbed into it and opened it wide;
you made a pact with those whose beds you
love,
and you looked on their nakedness.
⁹You went to Moloch^a with olive oil
and increased your perfumes.
You sent your ambassadors^b far away;
you descended to the grave^c itself!
¹⁰You were wearied by all your ways,

---

^a9 Or *to the king*   ^b9 Or *idols*   ^c9 Hebrew *Sheol*

but you would not say, 'It is hopeless.'
You found renewal of your strength,
and so you did not faint.

¹¹"Whom have you so dreaded and feared
that you have been false to me,
and have neither remembered me
nor pondered this in your hearts?
Is it not because I have long been silent
that you do not fear me?
¹²I will expose your righteousness and your works,
and they will not benefit you.
¹³When you cry out for help,
let your collection ⸢of idols⸣ save you!
The wind will carry all of them off,
a mere breath will blow them away.
But the man who makes me his refuge
will inherit the land
and possess my holy mountain."

Comfort for the Contrite

¹⁴And it will be said:

"Build up, build up, prepare the road!
Remove the obstacles out of the way of my
people."
¹⁵For this is what the high and lofty One says—
he who lives forever, whose name is holy:
"I live in a high and holy place;
but also with him who is contrite and lowly in
spirit,
to revive the spirit of the lowly
and to revive the heart of the contrite.
¹⁶I will not bring charges forever,
nor will I always be angry;
for then the spirit of man would grow faint
before me—

the breath of man that I have created.
¹⁷I was enraged by his sinful greed;
so I punished him, and hid my face in anger,
yet he kept on in his willful ways.
¹⁸I have seen his ways, but I will heal him;
I will guide him and restore comfort to him,
¹⁹   creating praise on the lips of the mourners in
Israel.
Peace, peace, to those far and near,"
says the LORD. "And I will heal them."
²⁰But the wicked are like the tossing sea,
which cannot rest,
whose waves cast up mire and mud.
²¹"There is no peace," says my God, "for the
wicked."

True Fasting

58 "Shout it aloud, do not hold back!
Raise your voice like a trumpet.
Declare to my people their rebellion
and to the house of Jacob their sins.
²For day after day they seek me out;
they seem eager to know my ways,
as if they were a nation that does what is right
and has not forsaken the commands of its God.
They ask me for just decisions
and seem eager for God to come near them.
³'Why have we fasted,' they say,
'and you have not seen it?
Why have we humbled ourselves,
and you have not noticed?'

"Yet on the day of your fasting, you do as you
please,

and you exploit all your workers.
⁴Your fasting ends in quarreling and strife,
and in striking each other with wicked fists.
You cannot fast as you do today
and expect your voice to be heard on high.
⁵Is this the kind of fast I have chosen,
only a day for a man to humble himself?
Is it only for bowing one's head like a reed
and for lying on sackcloth and ashes?
Is that what you call a fast,
a day acceptable to the LORD?

⁶"Is not this the kind of fasting I have chosen:
to loose the chains of injustice
and untie the cords of the yoke,
to set the oppressed free
and break every yoke?
⁷Is it not to share your food with the hungry
and to provide the poor wanderer with
shelter—
when you see the naked, to clothe him,
and not to turn away from your own flesh and
blood?
⁸Then your light will break forth like the dawn,
and your healing will quickly spring up;
then your righteousnessᵃ will go before you,
and the glory of the LORD will be your rear
guard.
⁹Then you will call, and the LORD will answer;
you will cry for help, and he will say: Here I am!

"If you do away with the yoke of oppression,
with the pointing finger and malicious talk,
¹⁰and if you spend yourselves on behalf of the
hungry

ᵃ 8 Or *your righteous One*

and satisfy the needs of the oppressed,
then your light will rise in the darkness,
and your night will become like the noonday.
¹¹The LORD will guide you always;
he will satisfy your needs in a sun-scorched
land
and will strengthen your frame.
You will be like a well-watered garden,
like a spring whose waters never fail.
¹²Your people will rebuild the ancient ruins
and will raise up the age-old foundations;
you will be called Repairer of Broken Walls,
Restorer of Streets With Dwellings.

¹³"If you keep your feet from breaking the Sabbath
and from doing as you please on my holy day,
if you call the Sabbath a delight
and the LORD's holy day honorable,
and if you honor it by not going your own way
and not doing as you please or speaking idle
words,
¹⁴then you will find your joy in the LORD,
and I will cause you to ride on the heights of
the land
and to feast on the heritage of your father
Jacob."
For the mouth of the LORD has spoken.

Sin, Confession and Redemption

59 Surely the arm of the LORD is not too short to
save,
nor his ear too dull to hear.
²But your iniquities have separated
you from your God;
your sins have hidden his face from you,
so that he will not hear.

³For your hands are stained with blood
    and your fingers with guilt.
Your lips have spoken lies,
    and your tongue mutters wicked things.
⁴No one calls for justice;
    no one pleads his case with integrity.
They rely on empty arguments and speak lies;
    they conceive trouble and give birth to evil.
⁵They hatch the eggs of vipers
    and spin a spider's web.
Whoever eats their eggs will die,
    and when one is broken, an adder is hatched.
⁶Their cobwebs are useless for clothing;
    they cannot cover themselves with what they
      make.
Their deeds are evil deeds,
    and acts of violence are in their hands.
⁷Their feet rush into sin;
    they are swift to shed innocent blood.
Their thoughts are evil thoughts;
    ruin and destruction mark their ways.
⁸The way of peace they do not know;
    there is no justice in their paths.
They have turned them into crooked roads;
    no one who walks in them will know peace.

⁹So justice is far from us,
    and righteousness does not reach us.
We look for light, but all is darkness;
    for brightness, but we walk in deep shadows.
¹⁰Like the blind we grope along the wall,
    feeling our way like men without eyes.
At midday we stumble as if it were twilight;
    among the strong, we are like the dead.
¹¹We all growl like bears;
    we moan mournfully like doves.
We look for justice, but find none;

for deliverance, but it is far away.

¹²For our offenses are many in your sight,
    and our sins testify against us.
Our offenses are ever with us,
    and we acknowledge our iniquities:
¹³rebellion and treachery against the LORD,
    turning our backs on our God,
fomenting oppression and revolt,
    uttering lies our hearts have conceived.
¹⁴So justice is driven back,
    and righteousness stands at a distance;
truth has stumbled in the streets,
    honesty cannot enter.
¹⁵Truth is nowhere to be found,
    and whoever shuns evil becomes a prey.

The LORD looked and was displeased
    that there was no justice.
¹⁶He saw that there was no one,
    and he was appalled that there was no one to
        intercede;
so his own arm worked salvation for him,
    and his own righteousness sustained him.
¹⁷He put on righteousness as his breastplate,
    and the helmet of salvation on his head;
he put on the garments of vengeance
    and wrapped himself in zeal as in a cloak.
¹⁸According to what they have done,
    so will he repay,
wrath to his enemies
    and retribution to his foes;
he will repay the islands their due.
¹⁹From the west, men will reverence the name of
    the LORD,
    and from the rising of the sun, they will
        revere his glory.

For he will come like a pent-up flood
    that the breath of the LORD drives along.[a]

20"The Redeemer will come to Zion,
    to those in Jacob who repent of their sins,"
                declares the LORD.

21"As for me, this is my covenant with them," says the LORD. "My Spirit, who is on you, and my words that I have put in your mouth will not depart from your mouth, or from the mouths of your children, or from the mouths of their descendants from this time on and forever," says the LORD.

The Glory of Zion

60 "Arise, shine! For your light has come,
    and the glory of the LORD rises upon you.
²See, darkness covers the earth
    and thick darkness is over the peoples,
but the LORD rises upon you
    and his glory appears over you.
³Nations will come to your light,
    and kings to the brightness of your dawn.

⁴"Lift up your eyes and look about you:
    All assemble and come to you;
your sons come from afar,
    and your daughters are carried on the arm.
⁵Then you will look and be radiant,
    your heart will throb and swell with joy;
the wealth on the seas will be brought to you,
    and to you the riches of the nations will come.
⁶Herds of camels will cover your land,
    young camels of Midian and Ephah.
And all from Sheba will come,
    bearing gold and incense

---

a 19 Or *When the enemy comes in like a flood,*
    the Spirit of the LORD will put him to flight.

and proclaiming the praise of the Lord.
⁷All Kedar's flocks will be gathered to you,
    the rams of Nebaioth will serve you;
they will be accepted as offerings on my altar,
    and I will adorn my glorious temple.

⁸"Who are these that fly along like clouds,
    like doves to their nests?
⁹Surely the islands look to me;
    in the lead are the ships of Tarshish,
bringing your sons from afar,
    with their silver and gold,
to the honor of the Lord your God,
    the Holy One of Israel,
    for he has endowed you with splendor.

¹⁰"Foreigners will rebuild your walls,
    and their kings will serve you.
Though in anger I struck you,
    in favor I will show you compassion.
¹¹Your gates will always stand open,
    they will never be shut, day or night,
so that men may bring you the wealth of the
    nations—
    their kings led in triumphal procession.
¹²For the nation or kingdom that will not serve
    you will perish;
    it will be utterly ruined.

¹³"The glory of Lebanon will come to you,
    the pine, the fir and the cypress together,
to adorn the place of my sanctuary;
    and I will glorify the place of my feet.
¹⁴The sons of your oppressors will come bowing
    before you;
    all who despise you will bow down at your
    feet

and will call you The City of the LORD,
    Zion of the Holy One of Israel.

¹⁵"Although you have been forsaken and hated,
    with no one traveling through,
I will make you the everlasting pride
    and the joy of all generations.
¹⁶You will drink the milk of nations
    and be nursed at royal breasts.
Then you will know that I, the LORD, am your
      Savior,
    your Redeemer, the Mighty One of Jacob.
¹⁷Instead of bronze I will bring you gold,
    and silver in place of iron.
Instead of wood I will bring you bronze,
    and iron in place of stones.
I will make peace your governor
    and righteousness your ruler.
¹⁸No longer will violence be heard in your land,
    nor ruin or destruction within your borders,
but you will call your walls Salvation
    and your gates Praise.
¹⁹The sun will no more be your light by day,
    nor will the brightness of the moon shine on
      you,
for the LORD will be your everlasting light,
    and your God will be your glory.
²⁰Your sun will never set again,
    and your moon will wane no more;
the LORD will be your everlasting light,
    and your days of sorrow will end.
²¹Then will all your people be righteous
    and they will possess the land forever.
They are the shoot I have planted,
    the work of my hands,
    for the display of my splendor.
²²The least of you will become a thousand,

the smallest a mighty nation.
I am the Lord;
in its time I will do this swiftly."

The Year of the LORD's Favor

61 The Spirit of the Sovereign Lord is on me,
because the Lord has anointed me
to preach good news to the poor.
He has sent me to bind up the broken-hearted,
to proclaim freedom for the captives
and recovery of sight*ᵃ* for the prisoners,*ᵇ*
²to proclaim the year of the Lord's favor
and the day of vengeance of our God,
to comfort all who mourn,
³ and provide for those who grieve in Zion—
to bestow on them a crown of beauty
instead of ashes,
the oil of gladness
instead of mourning,
and a garment of praise
instead of a spirit of despair.
So they will be called oaks of righteousness,
a planting of the Lord
for the display of his splendor.

⁴They will rebuild the ancient ruins
and restore the places long devastated;
they will renew the ruined cities
that have been devastated for generations.
⁵Aliens will shepherd your flocks;
foreigners will work your fields and vineyards.
⁶But you will be called priests of the Lord,
you will be named ministers of our God.
You will feed on the wealth of nations,
and in their riches you will boast.

*ᵃ*1 Or *and release*   *ᵇ*1 Hebrew; Septuagint *the blind*

⁷Instead of their shame
    my people will receive a double portion,
and instead of disgrace
    they will rejoice in their inheritance;
and so they will inherit a double portion in their
        land,
    and everlasting joy will be theirs.

⁸"For I, the LORD, love justice;
    I hate robbery and iniquity.
In my faithfulness I will reward them
    and make an everlasting covenant with them.
⁹Their descendants will be known among the
        nations,
    and their offspring among the peoples.
All who see them will acknowledge
    that they are a people the LORD has blessed."

¹⁰I delight greatly in the LORD;
    my soul rejoices in my God.
For he has clothed me with garments of salvation
    and arrayed me in a robe of righteousness,
as a bridegroom adorns his head, like a priest,
    and as a bride adorns herself with her jewels.
¹¹For as the soil makes the sprout come up
    and a garden causes seeds to grow,
so the Sovereign LORD will make righteousness
        and praise
    spring up before all nations.

Zion's New Name

62 For Zion's sake I will not keep silent;
    for Jerusalem's sake I will not remain quiet,
till her righteousness shines out like the dawn,
    her salvation like a blazing torch.
²The nations will see your righteousness,
    and all kings your glory;

you will be called by a new name
    that the mouth of the LORD will bestow.
³You will be a crown of splendor in the LORD's
    hand,
    a royal diadem in the hand of your God.
⁴No longer will they call you Deserted,
    or name your land Desolate.
But you will be called Hephzibah,ᵃ
    and your land Beulahᵇ;
for the LORD will take delight in you,
    and your land will be married.
⁵As a young man marries a maiden,
    so will your sons marry you;
as a bridegroom rejoices over his bride,
    so will your God rejoice over you.

⁶I have posted watchmen on your walls,
    O Jerusalem;
    they will never be silent day or night.
You who call on the LORD,
    give yourselves no rest,
⁷and give him no rest till he establishes Jerusalem
    and makes her the praise of the earth.

⁸The LORD has sworn by his right hand
    and by his mighty arm;
"Never again will I give your grain
    as food for your enemies,
and never again will foreigners drink the new
    wine
    for which you have toiled;
⁹but those who harvest it will eat it
    and praise the LORD,
and those who gather the grapes will drink it
    in the courts of my sanctuary."

ᵃ4 *Hephzibah* means *my delight is in her.*   ᵇ4 *Beulah* means *married.*

¹⁰Pass through, pass through the gates!
    Prepare the way for the people.
Build up, build up the highway!
    Remove the stones.
Raise a banner for the nations.

¹¹The LORD has made proclamation
    to the ends of the earth:
"Say to the Daughter of Zion,
    'See, your Savior comes!
See, his reward is with him,
    and his recompense accompanies him.' "
¹²They will be called The Holy People,
    The Redeemed of the LORD;
and you will be called Sought After,
    The City No Longer Deserted.

God's Day of Vengeance and Redemption

63 Who is this coming from Edom,
    from Bozrah, with his garments stained
        crimson?
Who is this, robed in splendor,
    striding forward in the greatness of his
        strength?

"It is I, speaking in righteousness,
    mighty to save."

²Why are your garments red,
    like those of one treading the winepress?

³"I have trodden the winepress—alone;
    from the nations no one was with me.
I trampled them in my anger
    and trod them down in my wrath;
their blood spattered my garments,
    and I stained all my clothing.
⁴For the day of vengeance was in my heart,

and the year of my redemption has come.
⁵I looked, but there was no helper,
      I was appalled that no one gave support;
   so my own arm worked salvation for me,
      and my own wrath sustained me.
⁶I trampled the nations in my anger;
      in my wrath I made them drunk
      and poured their blood on the ground."

Praise and Prayer

⁷I will tell of the kindnesses of the LORD,
      the deeds for which he is to be praised,
      according to all the LORD has done for us—
   yes, the many good things he has done
      for the house of Israel,
      according to his compassion and many
         kindnesses.
⁸He said, "Surely they are my people,
      sons who will not be false to me";
   and so he became their Savior.
⁹In all their distress he too was distressed,
      and the angel of his presence saved them.
   In his love and mercy he redeemed them;
      he lifted them up and carried them
      all the days of old.
¹⁰Yet they rebelled
      and grieved his Holy Spirit.
   So he turned and became their enemy
      and he himself fought against them.

¹¹Then they recalled[a] the days of old,
      of Moses and his people—
   Where is he who brought them through the sea,
      with the shepherd of his flock?

---

[a] 11 Or *But may he recall*

Where is he who set
  his Holy Spirit among them,
¹²who sent his glorious arm of power
  to be at Moses' right hand,
who divided the waters before them,
  to gain for himself everlasting renown,
¹³and who led them through the depths?
Like a horse in open country,
  they did not stumble;
¹⁴like cattle that go down to the plain,
  they were given rest by the Spirit of the LORD.
This is how you guided your people,
  to make for yourself a glorious name.

¹⁵Look down from heaven and see,
  from your lofty throne, holy and glorious.
Where are your zeal and your might?
  Your tenderness and compassion are withheld
    from us.
¹⁶But you are our Father,
  though Abraham does not know us
  or Israel acknowledge us;
you, O LORD, are our Father,
  our Redeemer from of old is your name.
¹⁷Why, O LORD, do you make us wander from
    your ways,
  and harden our hearts so we do not revere
    you?
Return, for the sake of your servants,
  the tribes that are your inheritance.
¹⁸For a little while your people possessed your
    holy place,
  but now our enemies have trampled down
    your sanctuary.
¹⁹We are yours from of old;
  you have not ruled over them,

they have not been called by your name.[a]

64 Oh, that you would rend the heavens and come
down,
that the mountains would tremble before
you,
[2]as when fire sets twigs ablaze
and causes water to boil—
come down to make your name known to your
enemies,
and cause the nations to quake before you!
[3]For when you did awesome things that we did
not expect,
you came down, and the mountains trembled
before you.
[4]Since ancient times no one has heard,
no ear has perceived,
no eye has seen any God besides you
who acts on behalf of those who wait for him.
[5]You come to the help of those who gladly do
right,
who remember your ways.
But when we continued to sin against them,
you were angry.
How then can we be saved?
[6]All of us have become like one who is unclean,
and all our righteousness is like filthy rags;
we all shrivel up like a leaf,
and like the wind our sins sweep us away.
[7]No one calls on your name
or strives to lay hold of you;
for you have hidden your face from us
and made us waste away because of our
sins.

[a] 19 Or *We are like those you have never ruled,*
like those never called by your name.

⁸Yet, O Lᴏʀᴅ, you are our Father.
>   We are the clay, you are the potter;
>   we are all the work of your hand.
⁹Do not be angry beyond measure, O Lᴏʀᴅ;
>   do not remember our sins forever.
> Oh, look upon us, we pray,
>   for we are all your people.
¹⁰Your sacred cities have become a desert;
>   even Zion is a desert, Jerusalem a desolation.
¹¹Our holy and glorious temple, where our fathers
>   praised you,
>   has been burned with fire,
>   and all that we treasured lies in ruins.
¹²After all this, O Lᴏʀᴅ, will you hold yourself
>   back?
>   Will you keep silent and punish us beyond
>   measure?

Judgment and Salvation

65 "I revealed myself to those who did not ask for
>   me,
>   I was found by those who did not seek me.
> To a nation that did not call on my name,
>   I said, 'Here I am, here I am!'
²All day long I have held out my hands
>   to an obstinate people,
> who walk in ways not good,
>   pursuing their own imaginations—
³a people who continually provoke me
>   to my very face,
> offering sacrifices in gardens
>   and burning incense on altars of brick,
⁴who sit among the graves
>   and spend their nights keeping secret vigil,
> who eat the flesh of pigs,
>   and whose pots hold broth of unclean meat,
⁵who say, 'Keep away; don't come near me,

for I am too sacred for you!'
Such people are smoke in my nostrils,
    a fire that keeps burning all day.

⁶"See, it stands written before me:
    I will not keep silent but will pay back in full;
    I will pay it back into their laps—
⁷both your sins and the sins of your fathers,"
    says the LORD.
"Because they burned sacrifices on the mountains
    and defied me on the hills,
I will measure into their laps
    the full payment for their former deeds."

⁸This is what the LORD says:

"As when juice is still found in a cluster of
      grapes
    and men say, 'Don't destroy it,
    there is yet some good in it,'
so will I do on behalf of my servants;
    I will not destroy them all.
⁹I will bring forth descendants from Jacob,
    and from Judah those who will possess my
      mountains;
my chosen people will inherit them,
    and there will my servants live.
¹⁰Sharon will become a pasture for flocks,
    and the Valley of Achor a resting place for
      herds,
for my people who seek me.

¹¹"But as for you who forsake the LORD
    and forget my holy mountain,
who spread a table for fortune
    and fill bowls of mixed wine for Destiny,
¹²I will destine you for the sword,
    and you will all bend down for the slaughter;

for I called but you did not answer,
I spoke but you did not listen.
You did evil in my sight
and chose what displeases me."

¹³Therefore this is what the Sovereign LORD says:

"My servants will eat,
but you will go hungry;
my servants will drink,
but you will go thirsty;
my servants will rejoice,
but you will be put to shame.
¹⁴My servants will sing
out of the joy of their hearts,
but you will cry out
from anguish of heart
and wail in brokenness of spirit.
¹⁵You will leave your name
to my chosen ones as a curse;
the Sovereign LORD will put you to death,
but to his servants he will give another
name.
¹⁶Whoever invokes a blessing in the land
will do so by the God of truth;
he who takes an oath in the land
will swear by the God of truth.
For the former troubles will be forgotten
and hidden from my eyes.

New Heavens and a New Earth

¹⁷"Behold, I will create
new heavens and a new earth.
The former things will not be remembered,
nor will they come to mind.
¹⁸But be glad and rejoice forever
in what I will create,
for I will create Jerusalem to be a delight

and its people a joy.
¹⁹I will rejoice over Jerusalem
and take delight in my people;
the sound of weeping and of crying
will be heard in it no more.

²⁰"Never again will there be in it
an infant that lives but a few days;
or an old man who does not live out his
years;
he who dies at a hundred
will be thought a mere youth;
he who fails to reach a hundred
will be considered accursed.
²¹They will build houses and dwell in them;
they will plant vineyards and eat their fruit.
²²No longer will they build houses and others
dwell in them,
or plant and others eat.
For as the days of a tree,
so will be the days of my people;
my chosen ones will long enjoy
the works of their hands.
²³They will not toil in vain
or bear children doomed to misfortune;
for they will be a people blessed by the LORD,
they and their descendants with them.
²⁴Before they call I will answer;
while they are yet speaking I will hear.
²⁵The wolf and the lamb will feed together,
and the lion will eat straw like the ox,
but dust will be the serpent's food.
They will neither harm nor destroy
in all my holy mountain,"
says the LORD.

Judgment and Hope

66 This is what the LORD says:

"Heaven is my throne
   and the earth is my footstool.
Where is the house you will build for me?
   Where will my resting place be?
²Has not my hand made all these things,
   and so they came into being,"
                                 declares the LORD.

"This is the one I esteem:
   he who is humble and contrite in spirit,
   and trembles at my word.
³But whoever sacrifices a bull
   is like one who kills a man,
and whoever offers a lamb,
   like one who breaks a dog's neck;
whoever makes a grain offering
   is like one who presents pig's blood,
and whoever burns memorial incense,
   like one who worships an idol.
They have chosen their own ways,
   and their souls delight in their abominations;
⁴so I also will choose harsh treatment for them
   and will bring upon them what they dread.
For when I called, no one answered,
   when I spoke, no one listened.
They did evil in my sight
   and chose what displeases me."

⁵Hear the word of the LORD,
   you who tremble at his word:
"Your brothers, who hate you
   and exclude you because of my name, have said,
'Let the LORD be glorified,

that we may see your joy!'
Yet they will be put to shame.
⁶Hear that uproar from the city,
hear that noise from the temple!
It is the sound of the LORD
repaying his enemies all they deserve.

⁷"Before she goes into labor,
she gives birth;
before the pains come upon her,
she delivers a son.
⁸Who has ever heard of such a thing?
Who has ever seen such things?
Can a country be born in a day,
or a nation be brought forth in a moment?
Yet no sooner is Zion in labor
than she gives birth to her children.
⁹Do I bring to the moment of birth
and not give delivery?" says the LORD.
"Do I close up the womb
when I bring to delivery?" says your God.
¹⁰"Rejoice with Jerusalem and be glad for her,
all you who love her;
rejoice greatly with her,
all you who mourn over her.
¹¹For you will nurse and be satisfied
at her comforting breasts;
you will drink deeply
and delight in her overflowing abundance."

¹²For this is what the LORD says:

"I will extend peace to her like a river,
and the wealth of nations like a flooding
stream;
you will nurse and be carried on her arm
and dandled on her knees.
¹³As a mother comforts her child,

> so will I comfort you;
> and you will be comforted over Jerusalem."

> ¹⁴When you see this, your heart will rejoice
> and you will flourish like grass;
> the hand of the LORD will be made known to his
> servants,
> but his fury will be shown to his foes.
> ¹⁵See, the LORD is coming with fire,
> and his chariots are like a whirlwind;
> he will bring down his anger with fury,
> and his rebuke with flames of fire.
> ¹⁶For with fire and with his sword
> the LORD will execute judgment upon all men,
> and many will be those slain by the LORD.

¹⁷"Those who consecrate and purify themselves to go into the gardens, following the one in the midst of*ª* those who eat the flesh of pigs and rats and other abominable things— they will meet their end together," declares the LORD.

¹⁸"And I, because of their actions and their imaginations, am about to come and*ᵇ* gather all nations and tongues, and they will come and see my glory.

¹⁹"I will set a sign among them, and I will send some of those who survive to the nations—to Tarshish, to the Libyans*ᶜ* and Lydians (famous as archers), to Tubal and Greece, and to the distant islands that have not heard of my fame or seen my glory. They will proclaim my glory among the nations. ²⁰And they will bring all your brothers from all the nations, to my holy mountain in Jerusalem as an offering to the LORD, on horses, in chariots and wagons, and on mules and camels," says the LORD. "They will bring them, as the Israelites bring their grain offerings, to the temple of the

---

ª 17 Or *gardens behind one of your temples, and*   ᵇ 18 Septuagint; Masoretic Text
And I know their actions and their imaginations. The time is coming for me to
ᶜ 19 Septuagint *Put* (Libyans); Hebrew *Pul*

LORD in ceremonially clean vessels. [21]And I will select some of them also to be priests and Levites," says the LORD.

[22]"As the new heavens and the new earth that I make will endure before me," declares the LORD, "so will your name and descendants endure. [23]From one New Moon to another and from one Sabbath to another, all mankind will come and bow down before me," says the LORD. [24]"And they will go out and look upon the dead bodies of those who rebelled against me; their worm will not die, nor will their fire be quenched, and they will be loathsome to all mankind."